MW00425775

"*Discover Your Gifts* is a must-read for anyone wanting to embrace their God-given gifts."

Erik Rees, author of *S.H.A.P.E.: Finding and Fulfilling Your Unique Purpose for Life*, cofounder of the Jessie Rees Foundation

"I plan to deploy this resource in my New York City congregation. Why? Because it is grounded in a biblical anthropology, rooted in solid catechesis, supported by data-driven analysis, and presented in a friendly format. Striving, in the power of the Spirit, to connect with our multiethnic, multilingual neighborhood and world, we need help. Everts's work shows us how our giftedness points us to the ultimate gift of Jesus' saving work."

John Arthur Nunes, pastor and former president of Concordia College New York

CELEBRATING
HOW GOD MADE YOU
AND EVERYONE YOU KNOW

DISCOVER YOUR Gifts

DON EVERTS
FOREWORD BY SAVANNAH KIMBERLIN

An imprint of InterVarsity Press
Downers Grove, Illinois

InterVarsity Press
P.O. Box 1400, Downers Grove, IL 60515-1426
ivpress.com
email@ivpress.com

InterVarsity Press® is the book-publishing division of InterVarsity Christian Fellowship/USA®, a movement of students and faculty active on campus at hundreds of universities, colleges, and schools of nursing in the United States of America, and a member movement of the International Fellowship of Evangelical Students. For information about local and regional activities, visit intervarsity.org.

Scripture quotations, unless otherwise noted, are from The Holy Bible, English Standard Version, copyright © 2001 by Crossway Bibles, a division of Good News Publishers. Used by permission. All rights reserved.

While any stories in this book are true, some names and identifying information may have been changed to protect the privacy of individuals.

All figures unless otherwise noted are designed by Annette Allen Studio; Gift icons by OX Creative; Data visualizations by Savannah Kimberlin and Alyce Youngblood, copyright Lutheran Hour Ministries.

The publisher cannot verify the accuracy or functionality of website URLs used in this book beyond the date of publication.

Cover design and image composite: David Fassett
Interior design: Jeanna Wiggins
Images: light blue abstract: © andipantz / iStock / Getty Images Plus
fine grain pattern: © GOLDsquirrel / iStock / Getty Images Plus
cardboard texture: © Katsumi Murouchi / Moment / Getty Images
flame illustration: © Pobytov / DigitalVision Vectors / Getty Images
abstract pattern: © Wako Megumi / iStock / Getty Images Plus
silhouettes of teens: © wundervisuals / E+ / Getty Images
acrylic abstract: © Wylius / iStock / Getty Images Plus

ISBN 978-1-5140-0373-2 (print)
ISBN 978-1-5140-0374-9 (digital)

Printed in the United States of America ∞

InterVarsity Press is committed to ecological stewardship and to the conservation of natural resources in all our operations. This book was printed using sustainably sourced paper.

Library of Congress Cataloging-in-Publication Data
Names: Everts, Don, 1971- author.
Title: Discover your gifts : celebrating how God made you and everyone you
    know / Don Everts.
Description: Downers Grove, IL : InterVarsity Press, [2022] | Includes
    bibliographical references.
Identifiers: LCCN 2021053193 (print) | LCCN 2021053194 (ebook) | ISBN
    9781514003732 (print) | ISBN 9781514003749 (digital)
Subjects: LCSH: Gifts—Religious aspects—Christianity. |
    Vocation—Christianity. | Gifts, Spiritual.
Classification: LCC BR115.G54 E94 2022 (print) | LCC BR115.G54 (ebook) |
    DDC 231.7—dc23/eng/20211115
LC record available at https://lccn.loc.gov/2021053193
LC ebook record available at https://lccn.loc.gov/2021053194

P 19 18 17 16 15 14 13 12 11 10 9 8 7 6 5 4 3 2 1
Y 38 37 36 35 34 33 32 31 30 29 28 27 26 25 24 23 22

DEDICATED

to the gifted thought

partners God gave me—

Ashley, Jason, and Tony

Contents

Foreword

SAVANNAH KIMBERLIN

Director of Research Solutions, Barna Group

A s I sat through the first planning workshop for this initiative with Lutheran Hour Ministries (LHM) two years ago, I quickly realized that researching the topic of giftedness was going to stretch me.

Considering my journey as a Christian to this point, I think it's fair to say I've invested significant energy in growing my faith over the years. However, at the start of this project, I soon realized I had a pretty big knowledge gap when it came to the topic of giftedness. To put it simply, I started with a limited understanding of the ways people can be called and designed for God's purposes. I remember being so moved by LHM's passion to see communities transformed through unleashed gifts that I jotted in my notebook, "Is my definition of calling too small? Of giftedness? Of vocation?"

Over the course of the next two years, this research took a jackhammer to my narrow definitions surrounding giftedness. I learned about my own gifts and about the collective power gifts can bring to a community when they're truly understood, activated, and celebrated.

I am thrilled that you have chosen to pick up this book and begin your own discovery journey. Here at the start, I would encourage you to pause for some self-evaluation, just as I did. Perhaps you also find yourself wondering if your definitions are too small, or maybe you're noticing you need to reevaluate how you view your own calling, giftedness, and vocation.

Our research suggests that many people are unsure of themselves when it comes to their gifts, skills, and abilities. Today, only half of US adults (46 percent) say they know or understand their own giftings well. Furthermore, among those who do understand their gifts, only 24 percent agree strongly that they are able to make good use of their giftings.

With this reality in mind, I invite you to allow this conversation to stretch your understanding of what giftedness really is—and what it means for your own life and community. I am so grateful for the ways it has stretched me. Indeed, everyone is a gift, everyone has gifts, everyone is called, and everyone can grow.

Introduction

SEEING BUZZ CLEARLY

I believe God made you and everyone you know as a gift with gifts to share.

Even though that's what the Bible says about us, I know it can be tempting to see ourselves and others very differently. And that's a problem. The reality is that the way we see ourselves and others directly affects how we feel and live life and treat each other. And that's why I've written this small book: to help us reckon with what the Bible says about how God made us and what he made us for.

I've also written this book to help us discover the unique gifts God has entrusted to each of us and to prayerfully consider how God might be calling us to use those gifts for his purposes in this world. It's incredible how so many hopeful paths open for us in life when we learn to see ourselves and others as God does: gifts with gifts to share. My stepfather, Buzz, helped me learn this in a way I'll never forget.

You should know I had a hard time loving Buzz when we first met. I tend to be a fairly loving person (I'm told), but from the beginning I found myself feeling stingy and annoyed, and acting a little mean toward Buzz.

Why? Well, by the time we met, Buzz was already married to my mom. And I can be a little protective when it comes to my mom. My mom is a saint; her small stature and humble demeanor and servant posture render her, in my eyes, a true gem. Buzz? When I first met Buzz, I'm not sure what surprised me more: his tattoos, his studded leather accessories, his nonstop corny jokes and smoking, or the fact that half of his body was paralyzed. Come to think of it, I was probably most surprised that he was married to my mom.

Would you think less of me if I told you that during our first time at a restaurant together, in Boulder, Colorado, I got so frustrated with Buzz's unending stream of unfiltered comments to people seated near us that I hid in the bathroom for over ten minutes just to collect myself? Well, there you have it. I had a hard time loving Buzz from the beginning.

Every single time I saw Buzz and his studded suspenders and gray goatee and crooked walk, I clenched up inside. My perspective on Buzz began to change, however, when he moved in with us.

REALLY SEEING BUZZ

A few years ago, my wife (Wendy) and I felt called by God to transform our garage into an apartment and invite Mom and Buzz and their cat, Winston, to move in with us and our three young kids. (I tell this story more fully in my book *The Spiritually Vibrant Home.*[1]) Looking back, I realize how much this move transformed my view of Buzz.

Don't get me wrong, Buzz was still Buzz—those of you who met him know what I'm talking about. *Quirky* is something of an understatement. And I was still me—stingy and annoyed and a little mean to Buzz from time to time. But living together 24-7 gave me these moments, these important windows of time, in which I was able to see Buzz differently.

One afternoon I was on the couch watching sports when I heard Buzz and my youngest, Victor, talking at the kitchen table. As I listened in to their conversation, I realized Victor had asked Buzz to read him one of his picture books, and Buzz was not reading the actual words but narrating a hilarious story based loosely on the pictures on each page. Victor smiled and giggled. And I realized how unique and creative Buzz's gift of gab could be. Weeks later, when Wendy and Buzz recorded an impromptu comedy show sitting at the same table, I laughed and laughed and began to realize that maybe I had misread Buzz.

The first time we had guests over after Mom and Buzz had moved in with us, Buzz insisted on showing them his collection of handmade jewelry, watches, and belt buckles before they left. He wanted them to choose one item to take with them as a gift. Initially these art pieces seemed bizarre to me, but our guests over the years loved them. I had to just smile and nod when I saw a new guest look surprised and honored to choose one.

Whether working on a home remodeling project or trying to fix something on my car, I found Buzz's unique suggestions for "MacGyver-ing" a solution to be pretty inspired and helpful.

Moment after moment, I was forced to reframe the way I saw Buzz. I had been so focused on his deficits that my view of him was wholly colored by what Buzz lacked, what Buzz couldn't do, and what Buzz did that inconvenienced me.

But then one of these moments would come along, and I could see that Buzz (for all his quirkiness) was actually delightful. Beautiful even. And considerably gifted. Over time I began to realize, in spite of my frustrations, that Buzz was actually *a gift with gifts to share*. It's difficult to overstate what a transformation in vision this was for me. It took living with Buzz to see this clearly. And what I saw surprised me.

The thing is, though, I shouldn't have been surprised at all. As we'll see in the coming pages, God's Word is clear on this matter: we are all wonderfully crafted by God. This is true of Buzz and me and you and everyone we know or will ever meet. We are all created as gifts with gifts to share.

In a sense, living with Buzz confronted me with an important aspect of biblical anthropology—what the Bible says about "the origin, nature, and destiny of human beings."[2] My view of Buzz (and everyone else, really) was transformed because I began to pay attention in a new way to an old truth: God made all of us fearfully and wonderfully. Sometimes returning to ancient, core truths like this can make all the difference in the world.

PUTTING FIRST ARTICLES FIRST

When I was going through confirmation in church as a young teenager, I had a lot of memorizing to do. Among the various verses of Scripture and formulations of doctrine I memorized were the Apostles' Creed and the Nicene Creed. Both are important theological summaries penned in the early generations of the Christian church.

These creeds follow a three-part trinitarian outline (what Christians believe about God the Father, God the Son, and God the Holy Spirit), but as an eighth grader my favorite part of each creed was unquestionably the first "article" about God the Father. This was not for deep or theological reasons but simply because the first article was the shortest. Let me show you what I mean. Here's the first article of the Apostles' Creed:

We believe in God, the Father Almighty,
Maker of heaven and earth.

And the corresponding article from the Nicene Creed:

> We believe in one God, the Father Almighty,
> maker of heaven and earth
> and of all things visible and invisible.

And that's it. Easy enough to memorize but, as it turns out, not so easy to believe or allow to affect our everyday lives. When I first met Buzz, for example, the last thing on my mind was that he had been made by God. I was focused instead on what I perceived to be his faults, and that directly affected how I treated him—stingy and annoyed and a little mean, remember? Living with Buzz, though, taught me that how we see people directly affects how we treat them. This is part of why the first article is so important.

You see, there is life-changing, relevant good news in this first article. Not good news about Jesus the Son (that's covered in the second article) but good news about God the Father. Good news that can prove to be just as liberating and life-enhancing for Christians today as it was when Martin Luther reacquainted the medieval church with this truth some five hundred years ago.

Luther was a Catholic monk whose studies kept pushing him further back in time to the original, core sources of Christianity. As he sought to go *ad fontes* (literally, "to the sources"), he encountered ancient, foundational truths that transformed his life. For example, consider how he reflected on the implications of the first article of the Apostles' Creed.

> I believe that God has made me and all creatures; that He has given me my body and soul, eyes, ears, and all my members, my reason and all my senses, and still takes care of them. He also gives me clothing and shoes, food and drink, house and home, wife and children, land, animals, and all I have. He richly and daily provides me with all that I need to support this body and life. He defends me against all danger and guards and protects me from all evil. All this He does only out of fatherly, divine goodness and mercy, without any merit or worthiness in me. For all this it is my duty to thank and praise, serve and obey Him. This is most certainly true.[3]

The first article is easy enough to memorize, but, as Luther's words remind us, its implications are deep and far reaching. It corrects our vision, helping us see ourselves differently and helping us see others differently too. It tells us that God made everyone (even Buzz) out of fatherly love, that "each person, no matter how wounded, has great dignity and the capacity to enrich others."[4]

Back in his day, Martin Luther knew that his contemporaries needed this kind of correction in vision. Luther lived in a medieval world where the religious (priests, nuns, and monks) were esteemed and all other Christians were looked down on as second-class citizens. And the way they saw each other affected how they treated each other. So Luther pointed the church back to their first-article beliefs.

In general, this was Luther's approach: he didn't suggest new ideas; instead, he invited Christians to reflect deeply on their core beliefs, including what they believed about how God made everyone. In practice this looked like Luther and his fellow Reformers reading afresh the good news in the Bible and helping the church gasp in delight. In this way Luther reintroduced liberating, life-enhancing doctrines to the church, one by one, helping Christians understand their everyday lives in light of God's Word.[5] As a result, Luther breathed new life and hope into Christians in Europe and, eventually, around the world.

Sometimes returning to ancient, core truths can make all the difference.

DISCOVERING YOUR GIFTS

In a small way, this sort of return is what happened to me when Buzz moved in. Living with Buzz not only allowed me to see him in a new (well, really old) first-article light, but it also challenged and refreshed how I look at everyone around me, including myself. I was confronted with the Bible's clear teaching, which we'll consider in the chapters ahead, that everyone is a gift with important gifts to share.

These old first-article truths turned out to be as powerful as they are simple.

I entered into a new season of this journey recently as I began to work with colleagues at Lutheran Hour Ministries on a new gift inventory called EveryGift. While I'm used to narrowly focusing on spiritual gifts entrusted to Christians, EveryGift Inventory looks at the gifts God has entrusted to all humans. It has helped me to better see and appreciate a much wider range of gifts.

This work on EveryGift eventually led to a new collaborative research project, conducted by Lutheran Hour Ministries and the Barna Group, focused on this richer, broader perspective of gifts. The findings from this nationwide study suggest that our postmodern moment is the perfect time to reengage with and reestablish these ancient, core, first-article truths about how God made us and entrusted us all with gifts (see this book's appendixes). As you'll see, we believe reclaiming a biblical view of ourselves and each other could have *ten beautiful implications* for us and our churches.

At the end of the day, reembracing a biblical anthropology carries with it an implicitly hopeful invitation to discover our gifts and share them with the world. As Paul wrote in his letter to the believers in Rome, "Having gifts that differ according to the grace given to us, let us use them" (Romans 12:6).

The reality is, you are a gift with gifts to share. James reminds us in his epistle that "every good gift" is given to us by our heavenly Father, a reality that ought to make us take these gifts seriously. God has given you gifts so you will use them. Kind of makes you want to discover all your gifts, doesn't it?

I invite you to join me in taking a look at what the Bible has to say about these gifts, specifically that

- God creates everyone as a gift imbued with dignity and worth.

- God entrusts everyone with important gifts.

- God calls everyone to use their gifts with purpose.

- God expects everyone to grow and develop their gifts.

- God calls every church to equip people to use their gifts.

I also invite you to explore what the EveryGift Inventory can help you discover (or remember) about yourself and those in your life. As I've experienced, hopeful paths open when you allow your inattentiveness to gifts or your narrow focus on spiritual gifts to be broadened by a comprehensive look at *every gift* God has entrusted to you and to those around you. But fair warning: this type of discovery can get personal, because it involves being honest about how we truly see ourselves and the people around us.

We will also consider the research findings in some detail and learn what unique obstacles and opportunities we face today when it comes to discovering our gifts. What specific barriers are keeping us from discovering, growing, and sharing our God-given gifts? And in what ways are we uniquely primed to discover our gifts and reap surprising fruits?

My own journey has convinced me that one of the most powerful works in any human's life is when they get more in touch with the good news that they are a gift with gifts to share, and so is everyone around them. Healthy self-esteem, a sense of purpose, genuine empathy, increased trust, growing power, recovered relevance, and fruitful engagement with our communities are just a few of the fruits that lie on the other side of that realization.

The good news is this: you are a gift with gifts to share. And so is everyone else you know. Let's spend some time discovering these gifts.

For you formed my inward parts;

you knitted me together in my mother's womb.

I praise you, for I am fearfully and wonderfully made.

Wonderful are your works;

my soul knows it very well.

KING DAVID, CIRCA 1000 BC
PSALM 139:13-14

In a summer season when the sun was mild

I clad myself in clothes . . .

Walked wide in this world, watching for wonders.

A fair field full of folk I found . . .

Of human beings of all sorts, the high and the low,

Working and wandering as the world requires.

WILLIAM LANGLAND, CIRCA 1370
PIERS PLOWMAN

There are no ordinary people.

C. S. LEWIS, 1942
THE WEIGHT OF GLORY

1

Everyone
Is a Gift

THE POWER OF SEEING PEOPLE
AS GOD SEES THEM

King David was writing psalms of prayer and praise three millennia before Lewis began writing his thoughtful Christian prose. And the poet William Langland was writing his influential masterpiece in the Middle Ages. But all three were profoundly struck when God allowed them to see people as he sees them.

David was offered a soul-altering vision of how God saw him as "fearfully and wonderfully made." Langland's protagonist wandered a medieval landscape looking for wonders, and his eyes were struck by humanity, a "fair field full of folk." And Lewis's awe-filled contemplation of humanity's immortal nature led him to the over-whelming conclusion that none of us will ever meet an "ordinary" human.

All three authors give testament to the fact that God sees every human he creates as a gift—a precious wonder imbued at their creation with dignity and worth. All three are reckoning with "the sacredness and dignity of the human person."[1] And all three point to the inevitable and beautiful implications of seeing ourselves and the people around us as God sees us.

How can you and I tap into the power that comes from seeing people as God sees them? And what are the practical implications that we will notice in our everyday lives if we do?

MY SOUL KNOWS IT VERY WELL

In Psalm 139 we get a sort of play-by-play of a conversation between David and God (we call this prayer) and, in a way, between David and himself (we call this thinking). David is wrestling with how God sees him, how God pursues him, and how God made him. David's words in the psalm reveal that he is not simply checking off a list of doctrines but is, instead, honestly reckoning with those truths. This includes the truth that God made David fearfully and wonderfully, knitting him together in his mother's womb.

These verses read not only like insightful anthropology but also like soulful autobiography. David is letting the reality that God sees him as a gift sink into his heart and his very soul.

"Wonderful are your works; my soul knows it very well" (Psalm 139:14).

The proclamation that his soul knows "very well" that he's a gift implies that there are different levels of knowing such a truth. Is it possible for our souls to know the truth of how "wonderful" God's works are not very well or meagerly or incompletely? If my soul is any indication, the answer is yes.

Before Buzz moved in with us, if you had asked me whether God loved and valued every human he'd ever created, I probably would have said yes. I may have even been tempted to back up that knowledge with Scripture ("For God so loved the world"). I knew that God loved his creation. I knew that he had formed every human who had ever lived. I had even read and treasured David's words in Psalm 139. But I'm not sure my soul knew that *very well* until Buzz moved in.

Living with Buzz caused this clear biblical anthropology to sink deeper into my heart. It confronted how meagerly and sporadically I believed this biblical view of humans, which David expressed so beautifully and which his heart "knew very well." I *knew* God loved people. But there was something about living with Buzz that helped me experience this truth at a deeper level. Michael Downey describes a similar lesson learned by those who work with adults with developmental or intellectual disabilities: "All theories of personality development and all philosophical explanations of human nature fade into an embarrassed silence when confronted with the stunning truth about the person that is learned from experience."[2]

My view of Buzz faded into embarrassed silence when confronted with God's view of him. And I've never forgotten, or quite recovered from, that lesson.

Just as David marveled that his frame was not hidden from God when he was being woven together in the womb, so I have learned to marvel that Buzz was not hidden from God either. God saw him as a gift, imbued with dignity and worth. And this, it turns out, is an important part of the anthropology the Bible reveals: every single human ever created is a gift.

EVERYONE IS A GIFT

We see this right from the beginning, where the opening chapters of the Bible are unambiguous: all humans are created by God. Genesis is clear that God was and still is the source of all life on earth, including every single human who has ever been created. There is only one Creator, and therefore all humans are fellow creations of God. As Luther put it, "I believe God has made me and all creatures." But humans, we're told, are special creations because, unlike everything else, humans are created in the image of God:

Then God said, "Let us make man in our image, after our likeness. And let them have dominion over the fish of the sea and over the birds of the heavens and over the livestock and over all the earth and over every creeping thing that creeps on the earth."

So God created man in his own image,
    in the image of God he created him;
    male and female he created them.
        (Genesis 1:26-27)

The repetition underscores the point: humans are not like other creatures. Human beings are special, marked out as different among all of creation. God created all life on earth, but only into humans does God breathe his own breath of life. As it's put a few verses later, "Then the Lord God formed the man of dust from the ground and breathed into his nostrils the breath of life, and the man became a living creature" (Genesis 2:7).

God's personal involvement in the creation of each human stops David in his tracks in Psalm 139. It changes David when he sees that God knit him together in his mother's womb. It is incredible to consider the personal care God has taken in his creation of every human who has ever lived. Every single person we will ever run into during our life has been formed and knitted by the Creator, intricately woven with great care by our God, whether or not they acknowledge him. There are no ordinary people, as C. S. Lewis put it.[3]

In fact, it is exciting (and a bit sobering) to consider that *Jesus himself* had a hand in crafting each one of us. The apostle John clarified this significant point about the work of Jesus, the Word, when he wrote, "He was in the beginning with God. All things were made through him, and without him was not any thing made that was made" (John 1:2-3; see also Hebrews 1:1-2; Colossians 1:16).

It is sublime to reflect on these passages as they reveal "the uniqueness and sacredness of each person."[4] As our souls begin to understand that everyone is a gift, two beautiful implications flower within us: our low self-esteem is confronted, and our habit of showing partiality is undercut.

BEAUTIFUL IMPLICATION 1: CONFRONTING OUR LOW SELF-ESTEEM

The good news that God sees everyone as a gift naturally delights many of us. But for some of us, this news flies in the face of a heavy assumption we have been lugging along with us every day of our lives: namely, that we are no gift. We are no wonder.[5]

I know this heavy assumption intimately. I lived the first twenty years of my life with the hard and fast knowledge (or so it seemed to me at the time) that I was different from everyone around me. I could see the wonder in others;

I could sense the dignity and worth imbued within them at their creation. But me? I felt different. I felt worthless. I felt unimportant.

I did not feel like a gift.

For anyone who struggles with low self-esteem, or even self-hatred, the news that everyone is a gift might seem laughable. Perhaps it's true that *everyone else* is a gift. But not me.

This broken and cracked self-perception is common in our fallen world. This is why it is so good that the Bible's clear anthropology confronts the heavy lie of self-hatred straight on. It's a kind of beautifully painful invasion for someone struggling with low self-esteem to be confronted, as David was, with the reality that we are each "fearfully and wonderfully" made.

How does God confront the self-downtrodden among us with this important truth? For David it was reflecting on God's goodness and power as a Creator. For me it was encountering God's affection and love for me in Jesus' sacrifice on the cross. At least that was the start. Healing is not always quick or immediate. It takes time for our souls to know this good news very well.

In my case, God confronted my self-hatred again and again, blow after blow. Each time, God's truth took deeper root and the twisted lie of my worthlessness lost ground. That lie lost ground as I read God's Word. It lost

ground as I prayed to God. It lost ground as I began journaling and confronted head-on the unexamined lies I
had been carrying within me. I remember how it lost
ground in significant ways as I mentored a younger
Christian who also struggled with low self-esteem. That
person's wonder and dignity and worth were so clear to
me, it was so obvious that God saw them as a gift . . . and
as I confronted them with this truth, I couldn't help but
know it at a deeper level for myself. Over time I became
able to genuinely cry out in prayer as David did: "Wonderful are your works; my soul knows it very well"
(Psalm 139:14).

In our broken and cracked world, it's understandable
that this confrontation takes time. You can't just snap your
fingers and have your soul know it very well. Think of
Gideon, patron saint of all those who struggle to see their
own wonder. When we first meet Gideon in the sixth
chapter of Judges, he has been brought low, with all his
fellow Israelites, by the ruthless Midianites. In modern
parlance, the Midianites are the high school bullies and
Gideon is the social outcast trying not to get noticed in the
halls of his high school. Gideon does not feel like a gift as
he awkwardly tries to beat out wheat in a cramped wine
press—anything to keep from being noticed by the Midianites, who will surely swoop in and steal his wheat and
lunch money if they notice him.

It's at that inglorious moment when an angel of the Lord appears to Gideon and confronts him with a glorious biblical anthropology: "The LORD is with you, O mighty man of valor" (Judges 6:12).

Oh, to have an angel look you in the eyes and call you a mighty person of valor! But Gideon's response? Well, sometimes it takes time for our twisted vision of ourselves to be displaced by God's vision of us. Gideon replies (to an angel of the Lord!), "Yeah, right," or something very close to that. But the angel, as God is always gracious to do, keeps confronting Gideon with the truth of his might and valor, inviting him to go and deliver his downtrodden fellow citizens. Gideon defends his low self-esteem, saying, "Please, Lord, how can I save Israel? Behold, my clan is the weakest in Manasseh, and I am the least in my father's house" (Judges 6:15).

Ah, Gideon. Low self-esteem can be stubborn in our fallen world, I know. But the Bible's clear anthropology is not going away, and God uses his Word (and whispers and times of prayer and journaling and mentoring relationships and angels and the extraordinary witness of Jesus' love for us on the cross) to confront the heavy lie of self-hatred straight on. And God patiently invades our lies and false assumptions with this simple but powerful truth: everyone is a gift.

RESEARCH INSIGHT: SOME PEOPLE
CAN'T SEE THEIR GIFTS

In our nationwide research, we wanted to know whether people are aware of and understand their specific gifts. To get a baseline, we asked people how many "giftings, skills, or abilities" they believed they had to share on a scale of 1–10, from not having any gifts to feeling they have a lot of talents to offer. We used multiple words (giftings, skills, abilities, talents) to purposefully invoke a wide range of gifts within people's minds—from those they were born with to those they've developed over time through practice. There was not a huge difference between practicing Christians and all US adults in their answers: on average, people responded around 6.4 on a scale of 1 to 10.[6]

When the data is analyzed based on education level and overall socioeconomic status, a difference is evident: on average, a higher education and higher socioeconomic status correspond with a slightly higher self-assessment of gifts.[7]

Time to Reflect

On a scale of 1 to 10, from not having any gifts to feeling you have a lot of talents to share, how would you rate your own giftedness?

A more illuminating finding came from analyzing the group of respondents who marked that they don't have any gifts, skills, or abilities to share. Consider this group of people that made up 3.5 percent of all respondents. What exactly is going on with this "no gift" group of people? As the researchers put it: "While the sample size of this group is too small to do an in-depth analysis . . . an overview of their answers provides some clues as to who these individuals are and why they might believe they are giftless."[8]

What are these clues that can help us understand this group? The first is demographic: those in this group are more likely to be older, unemployed, or at a lower socioeconomic level. It's not hard to imagine how such circumstances might conspire to make someone think they have no gifts, skills, or abilities.

But the most striking clue relates to how *disconnected* this "no gift" group of people appears to be:

- A large portion of them has not been to church in the last six months.

- About half of this group says they don't know any of their neighbors.

- They are less likely to have ever worked on a community project.

- They don't feel like they have a sense of community in their life.[9]

This evidence of disconnectedness stands in stark contrast, statistically, to those who identify at least one or more giftings in themselves.

What exactly do these findings tell us? Well, we can't say definitively that their lack of spiritual or community connections have *caused* them to see themselves as lacking any gifts, skills, or abilities. But being disconnected from church, community, and relationships may allow the heavy lie of low self-esteem to go unchallenged. I can personally attest to how God often used a passage of Scripture, a sermon on Jesus, or the people around me to confront and chip away at my own low self-esteem.

God patiently invades our lies and false assumptions with the simple but powerful good news that we are gifts. And he often accomplishes this patient invasion *through other people*. Giftedness lives most vibrantly in community. We need heralds in our lives who remind us of our own worth.

The plight of this disconnected "no gift" group underscores just how important it is for us to continue to champion this good news in our lives and in the lives of others. It seems unlikely that any person could see or appreciate their different gifts unless they first recognize, at a core level, their basic dignity and worth.

Time to Reflect

Who do you know that could use a friendly reminder that they are loved and valuable and, at their core, a wonder? How could you remind them?

BEAUTIFUL IMPLICATION 2: UNDERCUTTING OUR HABIT OF SHOWING PARTIALITY

The good news that God sees everyone as a gift may seem uncontroversial and life affirming. But for some of us this news undercuts a nasty (if unconscious) habit of seeing other people as worth less than we are, if not seeing some people as downright *worthless*. We may not be proud of this habit. We may not even be willing to admit out loud what we feel inside, but for some of us in this broken world, the idea that everyone is a gift flies in the face of our fallen habit of (as the Bible puts it) "showing partiality."

One of my mentors, Gene, experienced this confrontation in a profound way. Gene was one of my first spiritual heroes— I grew up in the faith listening and relistening to Gene's unforgettable sermons. But I was most impacted by observing the way he treated the people around him. Gene was so unhurried, so gracious, so attentive. It was as if whomever he was talking to was the most important person in the world. Gene's communication gifts were something to behold.

What a huge surprise, then, when Gene casually shared with me one day that he had grown up "elitist," as he put it. I was shocked, so I pressed for details. Gene explained that he was raised in rural Colorado and excelled early in life. He claimed he had read every book in the library of his small town before graduating from high school, and the more educated Gene became, the more elevated his tastes became. By the time Gene entered college, he was an elitist: he attributed worth to people based on their wealth, education, clothing, and standing in society. And he treated people accordingly.

How could a self-avowed elitist become someone who had such genuine grace and kindness toward people from all walks of life? The answer, in short: Gene's longstanding elitism was powerfully undercut by the Bible's clear anthropology. While exploring the Christian faith in college, Gene was confronted with the good news that God sees everyone as a gift.

It was while reading the Gospels, Gene told me, that he understood that to follow Jesus meant seeing people as Jesus did and treating them accordingly. Over time, God's truth about people displaced Gene's elitist assumptions—so much so that Gene's gracious, loving way with people became one of the most striking and memorable features of his life.

This same sort of transformation is something we all need. Since the fall of humanity and the entrance of sin into our world, we're all somewhat predisposed to elitism, though few of us would use that word to describe our views. We are tempted to treat certain people (or types of people) with dignity and respect, and to treat other people in lesser ways. We tend to look down our noses at some people—though who exactly those people are may change over time.

None of us are immune to this. I remember distinctly how easy it was, as someone who grew up poor, to look down my nose at rich people. We're all elitists of some sort. Paul points out this unfortunate habit even within the church where, at times, certain parts of the body look down on other parts of the body (1 Corinthians 12).

The Bible's language referring to this nasty elitist posture is "showing partiality." In the Bible we read that God doesn't show partiality (Job 34:19) and neither should we (Job 13:10; Proverbs 24:23; Proverbs 28:21). As it's put simply in Deuteronomy, "You shall not show partiality" (Deuteronomy 16:19). In the New Testament we hear the same call (1 Timothy 5:21; Ephesians 6:9) and are reminded that such a way of seeing people is a violation of God's law and constitutes having "evil thoughts" (James 2:1-13).

Consider Jesus' rationale when calling his disciples not just to love friends but also enemies:

> You have heard that it was said, "You shall love your neighbor and hate your enemy." But I say to you, Love your enemies and pray for those who persecute you, so that you may be sons of your Father who is in heaven. For he makes his sun rise on the evil and on the good, and sends rain on the just and on the unjust. (Matthew 5:43-45)

Jesus' view is clear: because God the Father shows no partiality, neither should his people. How we treat the people around us is a central part of our faith. Just as Gene understood all those years ago, to follow Jesus, who sees every human as a gift, is to have your way of treating people transformed.

Because we are all tempted to be elitists in our fallen world, we all need God to transform how we see and treat the people around us. As I witnessed in Gene and experienced myself while living with Buzz, this is something God loves to do. He can replace our broken, twisted, and elitist ways of looking at the people around us with a clear, clean, biblical vision. God can wipe away our confusion and help us see that everyone—regardless of class or creed, race or nation—is a gift. The latest research reveals just how important this change in vision is for Christians.

Nationwide research, conducted over four years (see appendix one), demonstrates a prominent gap in trust between Christians and non-Christians. For example, while studying how Christians relate with their neighbors, we

WHO IS BEST SUITED TO SOLVE
COMMUNITY PROBLEMS?

% RANKED THIS OPTION FIRST

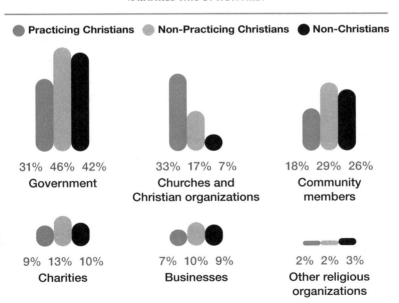

Practicing Christians   **Non-Practicing Christians**   **Non-Christians**

31% 46% 42%
Government

33% 17% 7%
Churches and
Christian organizations

18% 29% 26%
Community
members

9% 13% 10%
Charities

7% 10% 9%
Businesses

2% 2% 3%
Other religious
organizations

n=2,500 US adults, July 25–August 15, 2019.

FIGURE 1.1

asked community members across the United States who they think is best suited to solve problems in the community. As you can see in figure 1.1, non-Christians are more likely to trust the government, community members, charities, and businesses to help in the community than they are to trust churches and Christian organizations.[10]

Why do non-Christians have such a difficult time trusting Christians? While this is a complex issue, a big part of the answer is that Christians are perceived to be judgmental. Christians are seen as people who "show partiality," looking down their noses at others.

This posture is off-putting. While studying how people engage in spiritual conversations, we asked when people believe it is unacceptable to share views on religion. As figure 1.2 shows, the top answer given by the general population was, "If it's disrespectful or judgmental."[11]

In the same study, we noticed that people are more likely to feel they were disrespected in a spiritual conversation than to feel they showed disrespect, as you can see in figure 1.3.[12] People in our times are very sensitive to feeling disrespected or judged. Judgmentalism powerfully erodes trust between Christians and non-Christians.

Other studies have reported similar results. For example, when millennials who don't go to church were asked how they saw Christians, a strong majority replied "judgmental" (87%) and "insensitive to others" (70%).[13]

IT'S UNACCEPTABLE TO SHARE YOUR VIEWS ON RELIGION . . .

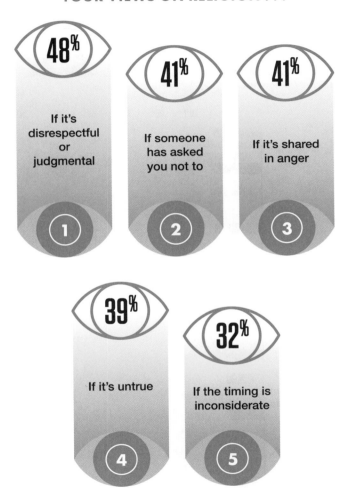

48%
If it's disrespectful or judgmental
1

41%
If someone has asked you not to
2

41%
If it's shared in anger
3

39%
If it's untrue
4

32%
If the timing is inconsiderate
5

n=1,070 US Adults, June 22-July 13, 2017.

FIGURE 1.2

MY MOST RECENT SPIRITUAL CONVERSATION

PERCENT AMONG US ADULTS WHO HAVE HAD A CONVERSATION ABOUT THEIR FAITH WITH SOMEONE WHO DOES NOT SHARE THEIR FAITH

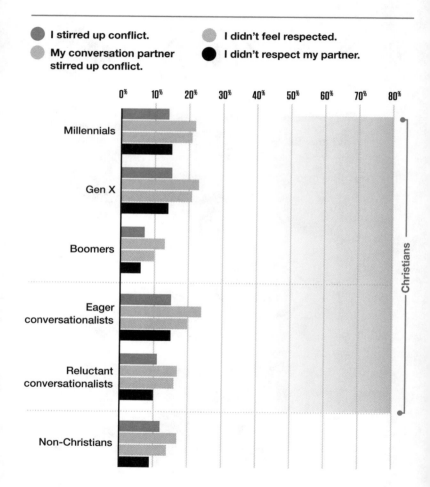

- I stirred up conflict.
- My conversation partner stirred up conflict.
- I didn't feel respected.
- I didn't respect my partner.

n=840 US adults who have had a conversation about their faith, June 22–July 13, 2017.

FIGURE 1.3

Time to Reflect

Do you feel the reputation of Christians as judgmental is fair or unfair? Have you ever felt distrusted simply because of your faith? If so, how did that make you feel?

While it may not be pleasant to be distrusted or seen as judgmental by the non-Christians in our lives, our discomfort should not be our greatest concern. Rather, we need to reckon with the reality that an unbelieving world that distrusts Christians is unlikely to listen to anything we have to say—including the good news about Jesus.

One practical way we can begin to rebuild trust and gain a hearing is to do what my mentor Gene did: allow the truth that everyone is a gift to confront our unexamined habit of showing partiality. If we confess our sins of showing partiality, if we begin to see people as God sees them, this will powerfully affect the way we treat the people around us. In the same way God transformed Gene from a self-avowed elitist to someone who had a gentle, affirming way of treating people, God can help all of us see and treat people more like he does.

Peter seemed to believe that showing respect to others was an important part of the Christian's posture both in society (1 Peter 2:18) and in the home (1 Peter 3:2), and was an important key for our spiritual conversations with non-Christians: "Always [be] prepared to make a defense to anyone who asks you for a reason for the hope that is in you; yet do it with gentleness and respect" (1 Peter 3:15).

This is what Gene did. Gene's gracious way with people gained him a hearing with hundreds of non-Christians over the years who he was then able to share the gospel with. Rather than grow embittered by the way people see Christians as judgmental, rather than consign ourselves to the margins of a society that values respect, let us allow the stunning truth that everyone is a gift confront our elitism. The result could be that we Christians gain a hearing, again, for the good news that we have to share with a hurting world.

Time to Reflect

What person (or group of people) are you most tempted to see as less valuable or look down on? Spend time confessing your sin of partiality to God, who is ready to extend grace, forgiveness, and healing.

SEEING PEOPLE AS GOD SEES THEM

From time to time after Buzz moved in with us, we would pack everyone into the minivan (my mom and Buzz, Wendy and me, and all three kids) and take the whole gang out to dinner at a restaurant.

We usually got great parking (Buzz came with a special parking pass) and a fairly large table. The seven of us would have a blast: eating lots of food, shooting straw covers at each other, talking and laughing. Predictably, Buzz would offer those seated near us and those serving us a steady diet of his corny jokes. And invariably we would leave a decent-sized mess and fairly large tip when all was said and done.

What a contrast these raucous restaurant outings were to that first time we took Mom and Buzz to a restaurant in Boulder, when Buzz's incessant comments drove me to hide for ten minutes in the bathroom just to collect myself. (In case you're curious: yes, I stranded Wendy at the table that whole time. Not a good move on multiple levels, I know.)

What a world of difference it makes to see someone clearly! It changes the game when we see people the way God sees them.

Living with Buzz helped the good news that everyone is a gift sink deeper into my soul. And spending the last year researching how people view giftings has convinced me of how important this kind of transformation is for all Christians.

May we all experience the power of seeing people as God sees them.

Next Steps

If you would like to tap into more of this power for yourself, here are some practical steps you could take:

OPTION 1: MEMORIZE PSALM 139:13-15.

> For you formed my inward parts;
>> you knitted me together in my mother's womb.
> I praise you, for I am fearfully and wonderfully made.
> Wonderful are your works;
>> my soul knows it very well.
> My frame was not hidden from you,
> when I was being made in secret,
>> intricately woven in the depths of the earth.

OPTION 2: REFLECT ON HOW YOU WERE MADE.

What Bible passages, experiences, interactions, relationships, or moments of prayer has God used to help you know you are a gift? Reflect on your own story and write in the heart what elements God has used to help you better understand that you are fearfully  and wonderfully made. Afterward, invite God to remind you of this truth by putting a sticky note on the mirror you use when getting ready in the morning that reads, "I am fearfully and wonderfully made!"

OPTION 3: REFLECT ON HOW THE PEOPLE AROUND YOU WERE MADE.
Who in your life (or your society) are you most tempted to look down on? As you get honest with your own temptation to show partiality, write in the heart the names of any individuals in your life, people in your culture (such as your least favorite politician), or types of people that you are tempted to see as less than valuable. Confess your elitism to God, then invite him to continue to undercut any inaccurate view you may have of others. Put a sticky note on your laptop or front door that reads "Everyone I interact with today is fearfully and wonderfully made!"

OPTION 4: FURTHER EXPLORE THE BIBLE'S TEACHINGS.
Read *Everyone Is a Gift: Letting God Transform How You See People*. I've written this booklet in conjunction with our research. It dives deeper into the theological underpinnings and practical implications of what we've explored in this chapter. It includes various reflection exercises to help our souls know *very well* what the Bible says about everyone being a gift. A beautifully illustrated companion booklet, *Precious in His Sight*, does the same for younger children. Go to lhm.org/gifted to find information about these booklets or download free digital and audio versions.

Every good gift and every perfect gift
is from above, coming down
from the Father of lights.

JAMES THE BROTHER OF JESUS, CIRCA AD 45
JAMES 1:17

Let that admirable light of truth shining
in them teach us that the mind of man,
though fallen and perverted from its
wholeness, is nevertheless clothed and
ornamented with God's excellent gifts.

JOHN CALVIN, 1536
INSTITUTES OF THE CHRISTIAN RELIGION

This means that every act of goodness,
wisdom, justice, and beauty—no matter who
does it—is being enabled by God. It is a
gift, and therefore a form of grace.

TIMOTHY KELLER AND
KATHERINE LEARY ALSDORF, 2012
EVERY GOOD ENDEAVOR

2

Everyone Has Gifts

THE POWER OF DISCOVERING THE GIFTS THAT GOD HAS ENTRUSTED TO US

During the Protestant Reformation, many important biblical teachings were reheard and reembraced by church leaders and Christians throughout the world. Famously, Martin Luther drew the eyes of Christians back to the biblical teaching that salvation is by grace through faith in Jesus. This core truth reminded Christians in a fresh way of both the glories of grace and the limitations of human effort.

One theologian of the time, known for his sober assessment of the limitations of human effort and our fallen nature, was John Calvin. Calvin's reading of Scripture led him to a pretty bleak view of the "total depravity of man," a sober doctrine that helps us understand the sheer beauty and grace of the salvation and sanctification found in Jesus.

Calvin is known for his unblinking lament of the state of "natural men" who don't have the "mind of Christ" (1 Corinthians 2:14). But just like his Reformation predecessor, Martin Luther, he was personally struck by the various gifts God had "bestowed indiscriminately upon pious and impious."[1] Calvin saw that everyone ever created has been gifted by their Creator with aptitudes, abilities, and skills.

The Protestant Reformation was a powerful time of reawakening to the ways God had "clothed and ornamented" everyday people (not just the religious) with gifts to use while on this earth. As Luther and others pointed out, there were powerful consequences to discovering the gifts God entrusted to us.

But how can you and I discover these gifts? How are these natural gifts that God has entrusted to all people different from the spiritual gifts Paul writes about in the New Testament?

EVERY PERFECT GIFT IS FROM ABOVE

The book of James, a letter from an early Christian leader (none other than the brother of Jesus), addresses a group of suffering Christians. James jumps right in at the beginning of the letter to address the "trials of various kinds" these Christians are facing. He recognizes that they need to know how to rightly think about and respond to the severe testing of faith they are experiencing.

The letter reads like a halftime locker room speech as much as it does careful doctrine. In this case, the Christians are the visiting team (James refers to them as "the twelve tribes in the Dispersion" [James 1:1]) and, with the suffering they are facing, it certainly feels like they are losing the game.

Early in the letter, James corrects the focus of these suffering Christians, telling them not to be deceived into thinking that God is a giver of bad things; rather, they are to focus on the glorious truth that God always gives good gifts. "Every good gift and every perfect gift is from above, coming down from the Father of lights" (James 1:17).

We can be like these suffering Christians. When times are tough, we tend to focus on deficits: the bad, the pain, what we're missing. We squint our eyes at God and accuse him of doling out bad things to us. Instead, James invites us to always focus, even in tough circumstances, on assets: the many good gifts God has bestowed on us. According to James, this is a powerful shift in perspective. Unfortunately, if my own eyes are any indication, this isn't always our first instinct.

Several years ago, some colleagues and I visited Buenos Aires, Argentina, to help square away logistics for a three-month ministry partnership between a US campus ministry and Argentine ministries in historically challenged communities. We had found the ministry site we were looking for in the middle of one of these *villas*—a cobbled-together set of buildings on a prominent corner of the community. Inside the ministry center we heard the sound of children and found out they were there for a tutoring program. They were eating what might be, we were told, the only meal they would get that day. The children seemed joyful, and the smell of fresh bread was a welcome break from the smell of garbage out in the street.

As we watched the children return to their lessons, the director of the ministry, Edilberto, walked in the door. He was a bear of a man—well over six feet tall, heavy, with a wide and genuine smile. But what was immediately striking about him was a large growth on the side of his neck, a growth that had to be a quarter of the size of his head. As I went to shake his hand, I noticed his humble clothes, worn flip-flops, and firm handshake.

After showing us the rest of the ministry center, Edilberto slowly walked us through the streets of the villa. As we walked and talked, I grew more and more impressed with him. Everyone we passed greeted him with obvious affection, and the comments he made about the community were insightful and strategic. He had grown up in this very villa, knew the place inside and out, and had profound strategic insights. Edilberto had significant interpersonal, leadership, and civic gifts.

At the end of the tour, we stood outside the ministry building to chat, and my heart was filled with hope. Hope for our partnership, hope for the villa. The shift in my heart from the beginning of the visit to the end was clear to me. You see, when we arrived in the morning, my first instinct was to immediately focus on the deficits of the community and of Edilberto. And the result? My heart had sunk. Any ministry led by someone with such pressing personal needs (like a large growth) was surely going to be hard-pressed to receive a team of college students for three months, let alone make a holistic difference in such a challenged community.

Boy, did I turn out to be wrong. "Do not be deceived, my beloved brothers" (James 1:16). These are the words James wrote to the squinty-eyed, suffering Christians, telling them to instead focus on the good gifts that come down from God. That's the exact correction I received that day when Edilberto took us on a walking tour of the villa. When I focused on deficits, my heart sank. When God helped me, instead, discover the various gifts with which God had clothed and ornamented Edilberto, my heart was filled with hope.

It turns out I needed the same halftime locker room speech as those early Christians of the dispersion. I needed to stop squinting my eyes and focusing on deficits. I needed to open my eyes wide to see the many good and perfect gifts God had entrusted to that community and director. This is an important nuance of the biblical anthropology we've begun to explore.

EVERYONE HAS GIFTS

We are told in the pages of the Bible that God not only sees everyone as a gift but also sees them as having gifts to share in a purposeful way. We see this inherent human purpose right from the beginning. In the Garden of Eden, God charges humans with a mission. He gives them work to do: "God blessed them. And God said to them, 'Be fruitful and multiply and fill the earth and subdue it, and have dominion over the fish of the sea and over the birds of the heavens and over every living thing that moves on the earth'" (Genesis 1:28).

Notice that right before God sends humans to do their work, he blesses them. This is a powerful action communicated with a powerful Hebrew word, *barak*, which means to "bestow power for success, prosperity, fertility."[2] God isn't just wishing humans well (how we tend to think of "blessing"); rather, he's actually bestowing on them power for success. He's entrusting into their hands the gifts and resources they will need to do the work he's sending them to do.

Why does God give humans these gifts? As Amy L. Sherman puts it in her book *Kingdom Calling: Vocational Stewardship for the Common Good*, "God has lavished all this on us for a reason: that we would use it for the common good, not for individual gain."[3]

The implications are important: people of every creed and no creed have talents, abilities, knowledge, and resources given to them by their gracious Creator, whether they realize the origin of those gifts or not. As Keller and Alsdorf point out, these good gifts are "a form of grace."[4]

Now, note that we are not talking specifically about "spiritual gifts" here. Spiritual gifts are those special abilities and empowerments given to Christians by the Holy Spirit that we read about in Paul's letters, such as wisdom, knowledge, faith, healing, miraculous powers, and prophecy (1 Corinthians 12:7-11). Rather, Genesis relates that God graciously gives gifts (we might call them "creaturely gifts" or "common gifts") to every human he creates.

Common gifts are not common in the sense that they are unimpressive or inconsequential, but in the sense that they are given to all. Just as God causes the rain to fall and the sun to shine on all people everywhere (Matthew 5:45), so God distributes "every good gift and every perfect gift" to all people everywhere—whether a physical skill, an intellectual aptitude, a creative flair, or a material blessing.

By God's grace, everyone has gifts "that differ according to the grace given to us" (Romans 12:6).

When I saw Edilberto walk in the room, I was tempted to focus on what he *lacked* (clean clothes, shoes, a healthy neck), and my heart sank. But when I took the time to discover the many ways he was *gifted* (with a thoroughgoing knowledge of the villa, rich relational connections in the community, wisdom for how to make a holistic difference, and mammoth strength of character and faith), my heart was filled with hope. This experience helped me understand why James encouraged the Christians in the dispersion to focus on God's good gifts.

When we begin to discover the many gifts God has entrusted to us, a variety of beautiful implications naturally results. Let's consider two together: a widening of our (too-narrow) focus on spiritual gifts and helping people discover previously unnoticed gifts.

BEAUTIFUL IMPLICATION 3: WIDENING OUR (TOO-NARROW) FOCUS ON SPIRITUAL GIFTS

The good news that everyone has gifts is a broad, beautiful, hope-filled piece of news. The more we learn to discover the gifts God has entrusted to us and to all those around us, the more hopeful and engaged we will likely become in putting those gifts to use in this world.

But a unique issue keeps Christians from paying attention to all these common gifts: our focus on spiritual gifts.

Paying attention to spiritual gifts is, of course, important. The apostle Paul helped the earliest Christians appreciate and fully embrace the blessings that come from spiritual gifts—those special abilities and empowerments given to Christians by the Holy Spirit. Paul's letters include lists of these gifts, guidance on how they are supposed to be used, and reflections on how Christians should think about and understand spiritual gifts. All of this emphasis on spiritual gifts is needed. As Paul wrote, "Now concerning spiritual gifts, brothers, I do not want you to be uninformed" (1 Corinthians 12:1).

It is not good to be *uninformed* about spiritual gifts. So there is nothing wrong with paying attention to spiritual gifts. But there *is* something wrong with focusing on spiritual gifts *to the exclusion* of any focus on common gifts. We can sometimes put so much emphasis on how to be faithful with the spiritual gifts God gives us that we ignore the many common gifts he has given to us. Or, even worse, we denigrate those common gifts.

When I was the director of a campus ministry in Colorado, I recruited and hired a lot of new campus missionaries. During one hiring cycle, Chris, a graduating senior, approached me. He had been very involved as a student leader, was a gifted engineering student, and a servant-hearted young man.

Chris had helped host and lead Bible studies and completed a summer-long mission trip. Chris approached me before graduation because he was interested in going on staff with our ministry.

We had several helpful conversations where we discussed Chris's considerable gifts and sense of calling and also the particular gift set required to be a campus missionary. While many good things came out of our times together, two things began to become clear to me as we had conversation after conversation: First, Chris's technical and critical thinking gifts seemed to point to a calling as an engineer. Second, he was convinced that his technical and critical thinking gifts were unimportant and the only things truly important and worthy were spiritual gifts and a ministry calling.

Never have I had to tell a single individual so many times that I was not going to hire them. Chris's persistence was commendable (he had always been a faithful, loyal young man), but the way he ignored and even denigrated the excellent gifts God had clothed and ornamented him with was lamentable. In the end, I'm glad to say, Chris was able to appreciate and embrace his gifts and use them powerfully for the common good, working faithfully as an engineer and an active member of the local church.

Sometimes our focus on spiritual gifts is too narrow and keeps us from fully appreciating all the gifts that have come down to us from our Father. Discovering our common gifts helps widen this narrow view.

RESEARCH INSIGHT: CHRISTIANS INVEST PRIMARILY IN DISCOVERING SPIRITUAL GIFTS

We wanted to know how much time and energy people are putting into discovering both their spiritual and common gifts. What did we find? In short, most of us aren't spending much time or energy thinking about the gifts we have received. As the researchers noted,

> While many people are familiar with assessments or tests that help them identify their unique talents, characteristics and abilities, most (68% of all US adults, 59% of practicing Christians) have not taken an assessment or test designed to help them better understand their giftings, abilities and talents. Only one in five US adults (21%) and three in ten practicing Christians (30%) have taken an assessment for this purpose.[5]

It was fascinating to discover, as you can see in figure 2.1, that more practicing Christians have taken such an inventory than individuals in the general population.[6]

We were also interested in finding out what is most often covered in gift inventories used by churches. So we asked pastors of churches that use such inventories what types of gifts they cover. As you can see in figure 2.2, almost all of these inventories covered spiritual gifts (97%). A much smaller percentage of pastors (71%) used inventories that also covered "practical giftings" that could be used in a church context, and even fewer (57%) focused on "practical giftings" that could be used outside the church.[7]

It would seem that, like my friend Chris, Christians come by their narrow focus on spiritual giftings honestly.

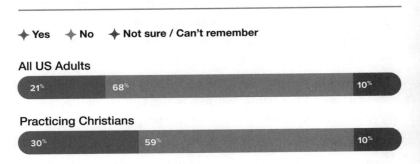

USE OF GIFTING ASSESSMENTS, INVENTORIES, OR TESTS

HAVE YOU TAKEN AN ASSESSMENT, INVENTORY, OR TEST THAT WAS DESIGNED TO HELP YOU BETTER UNDERSTAND YOUR GIFTINGS, ABILITIES, OR TALENTS?

◆ Yes   ◆ No   ◆ Not sure / Can't remember

All US Adults

| 21% | 68% | 10% |

Practicing Christians

| 30% | 59% | 10% |

n=1,504 US adults, June 16–July 6, 2020.
n=1,374 US practicing Christian adults, June 16–July 6, 2020.

FIGURE 2.1

As the researchers noted, "There's a good chance church-based assessment opportunities lean toward being spiritual in nature or for the benefit of the ministry."[8]

While it would appear that many churches are not in danger of being "uninformed about spiritual gifts," it is possible that our focus on spiritual gifts to the exclusion of common gifts has begun to affect what we pay attention to and value. We look for spiritual gifts because we value spiritual gifts. The fact that we so rarely look for common gifts undoubtedly diminishes how much we value them or think about them.

TOPICS COVERED WITHIN CHURCH GIFTING ASSESSMENTS

WHAT IS COVERED IN THESE "GIFTS INVENTORIES"? SELECT ALL THAT APPLY.

Base: pastors who say their churches take a gifts inventory

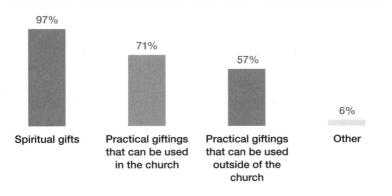

| Spiritual gifts | Practical giftings that can be used in the church | Practical giftings that can be used outside of the church | Other |
| 97% | 71% | 57% | 6% |

n=272 US Protestant pastors whose churches take a gifts inventory, June 23–July 28, 2020.

FIGURE 2.2

Time to Reflect

Have you ever taken an assessment, inventory, or test to help you better understand your gifts? If so, was the focus on spiritual gifts alone or common gifts as well?

BEAUTIFUL IMPLICATION 4: HELPING PEOPLE DISCOVER PREVIOUSLY UNNOTICED GIFTS

This good news—that everyone has gifts—is a seed of doctrine that wants to grow into full-bloomed curiosity. If everyone has gifts, well, then: What are my gifts? And what are my friends' gifts? And those in my household? And others in my church? And people I work with? If it really is true that God has clothed and ornamented every person he's created with excellent gifts, then let's discover what they are!

How God has specifically blessed each one of us is an indication of his purpose for our time on earth. This ought to drive us to discover all our gifts and those of the people around us.

For some of us, however, this curiosity does not come naturally. For all sorts of reasons there are those among us who feel ungifted. We aren't excited with curiosity about our gifts for the simple reason that over time we have come to suspect that when God was handing out excellent gifts he passed over us.

My Journey of Gift Discovery and the EveryGift Inventory

In the thirty years since I graduated from high school, I would guess I have taken more assessments, inventories, and surveys than the average American. I have had wonderful leaders in a variety of organizations who have helped me discover more about my temperament, work styles, spiritual gifts, and more. I would say I am a fairly self-aware person.

This is why I was sort of blindsided by how much I have learned about myself during the course of our research into gifts. I thought I knew all my gifts. In fact, I have been pretty purposeful over the years to make sure I am in roles and situations where I can be faithful to use the gifts God has entrusted to me. (I've always figured God gives us gifts so that we will use them.)

How unexpected, then, to take the EveryGift Inventory (that I myself had a hand in developing!) and find myself both surprised and excited when I got my personalized results back. I wasn't surprised to see that communication gifts and technical gifts (in writing and editing) were top gifts for me. These two gifts are pretty central to what I do most days.

TWELVE TYPES OF GIFTS

Entrepreneurial gifts *help you identify new opportunities, set goals, and design strategies to achieve them. Gifts include analytical thinking, market research, marketing skills, problem solving, and sales.*

Interpersonal gifts *help you interact with, care for, and build relationships with others. Gifts include active listening, self-awareness, and empathy.*

Technical gifts *help you perform specific tasks that require a special and refined set of skills. Gifts include craftsmanship, profession-specific knowledge, and acquired skills.*

Teamwork gifts *help you effectively collaborate with and work alongside others. Gifts include collaboration, communication, empathy, humility, positivity, and problem solving.*

Leadership gifts *help you organize people to reach a shared goal and effectively lead them toward that goal. Gifts include the ability to teach and mentor, flexibility, risk taking, team building, and time management.*

Communication gifts *help you communicate with individuals or groups in a clear and engaging way. Gifts include organization of thought, presentation, and storytelling.*

Management gifts *help you manage both tasks and people. Gifts include decision making, project planning, task delegation, and communication.*

Financial gifts *help you plan, organize, direct, and control financial activities. Gifts include accounting, planning, and attention to detail.*

Critical thinking gifts *help you process data to solve problems or make informed decisions. Gifts include analytical thinking, creativity, data analytics, and decision making.*

Artistic gifts *help you express yourself in creative and artistic ways. Gifts include all forms of artistic expression, media use, design, composition, and performance.*

Civic gifts *help you make an impact by participating as a citizen within an organized community. Gifts include advocacy, knowledge of political systems, and the ability to critically think about civic and political life.*

Intercultural gifts *help you relate to people from other cultures and social groups. Gifts include language skills, respect for others, and the ability to understand cultural differences.*

FIGURE 2.3

But the EveryGift Inventory (which explores twelve distinct areas of common gifts, as listed in figure 2.3) also helped me identify (and in some cases remember) that I also have been entrusted by God with leadership gifts, teamwork gifts, entrepreneurial gifts, and even some intercultural gifts. These results kicked off a wonderful, prayerful process in my life, considering if and how I should be using these other gifts more. Plenty of conversations with Wendy and close friends have helped me begin to reckon with what it would look like to be more purposeful to grow and share these other gifts. Taking a wider view than just my spiritual gifts or the gifts I'm most familiar with has had a powerful impact on my life and, I pray, will impact others as I share more of the gifts entrusted to me.

Unfortunately, some of us may have been told (explicitly or implicitly) that we are useless. Others of us may have gotten entwined in a twisted game of comparison in which we so focus and admire and long for the gifts of others that we're tempted to overlook or diminish our own. And as the book of James helps us see, it is also not uncommon for difficulties in life to cause us to squint our eyes and focus on the deficits all around and within us. There's nothing like a bad day or steep hill or season of struggle to make us wonder if, perhaps, we are ungifted after all (especially if we are gazing at others who seem to be sailing right along in life).

Regardless of the reason, there are many among us who need help discovering our gifts or even believing that there are gifts there to be discovered. If my experience with my oldest child, Simon, is any indication, this is a tender and powerful work.

Simon always struggled in school growing up, but those struggles seemed to intensify once he entered middle school. He began to wonder about his gifts or lack thereof. The basic landscapes of learning (listening in class, reading textbooks, writing papers, taking tests) all looked like treacherously steep hills for Simon, and he struggled mightily to make much progress. As he watched his friends and classmates breeze through assignments that took him hours to complete, Simon was tempted to believe he was ungifted. (Alas, it doesn't take much imagination to picture how such academic struggles interacted with other social, emotional, and physical landmines endemic to the middle school context.)

I'll never forget the day we got the results back on a variety of tests Simon's teachers and school counselors had requested. The school shared two important findings with my wife and me: first, Simon was extraordinarily gifted intellectually (his IQ was off the charts); and second, he had a learning disability (dysgraphia) that made certain academic tasks super tough for Simon and also made it difficult for teachers to assess his learning.

Armed with this knowledge, we sat down with Simon on our living room couch. I told him, "Simon, we got results from those tests, and they confirmed two things we've known all along. You are really smart. And school is really hard for you." As we told him about the specific findings, tears started streaming down his face. With practiced doubt in his voice but a small seed of hope in his eyes, he asked, "You mean I'm gifted?"

"Yes, Simon. You are gifted!" Simon's academic struggles may have led him to temporarily believe otherwise, but God has clothed and ornamented Simon with excellent gifts to use with purpose in his life—including financial, technical, teamwork, leadership, and entrepreneurial gifts!

School didn't become easy at that point, but Simon was able to tackle high school and college, and even started his own small business with the assurance that he was, indeed, entrusted by God with gifts.

How many of us need to be sat down on a couch and told the same thing: we are gifted! Not only are we fearfully and wonderfully made by God, but part of knitting us together was blessing us (*barak*) with various aptitudes, abilities, and skills to use with purpose during our time on earth. As Gene Edward Veith put it,

> God—making use of your family and your culture—created you as you are. . . . Thus you have particular talents, which you are to understand are His gifts. You have a particular personality, with interests, likes, and dislikes that not everyone shares. Such is the plenitude of God's creation that no two people—or snowflakes or leaves or anything God has made—are exactly alike.[9]

Reckoning with these ideas may cause some of us to embrace, perhaps for the first time in our lives, that we are, indeed, uniquely gifted. And for all of us it should fuel a hopeful curiosity to discover and be intentional with our various gifts.

RESEARCH INSIGHT: MEN AND WOMEN EXPERIENCE DISCOVERING GIFTS DIFFERENTLY

The journey of discovering our gifts is unique for each person. Our findings reveal that this experience tends to differ between men and women. For example, while 41 percent of practicing Christian men believe it is "very important" to identify their gifts, only 33 percent of practicing Christian women reported the same.[10] Among practicing Christians, men are also more likely than women to say they know their giftings, abilities, and skills "extremely well" or "very well" (fig. 2.4).[11]

Given these gender discrepancies, is it any surprise to find that, on average, men report having a slightly higher level of giftedness than women?[12] Why exactly does this gender discrepancy exist? This is a large and important question to ask. Christian authors like Katelyn Beaty and Margot Starbuck have done an excellent job of naming the various internal and external, subtle and overt, emotional and sociological realities that women navigate today.[13] While our findings don't shine a light on these important issues, they do raise

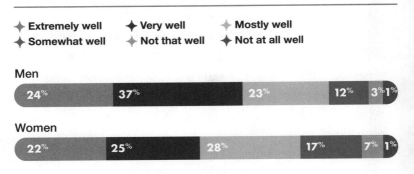

KNOWING AND UNDERSTANDING INDIVIDUAL GIFTINGS, BY GENDER

HOW WELL WOULD YOU SAY YOU KNOW YOUR OWN GIFTINGS, ABILITIES, OR SKILLS?

Percent among practicing Christians

◆ Extremely well   ◆ Very well   ◆ Mostly well
◆ Somewhat well   ◆ Not that well   ◆ Not at all well

Men

| 24% | 37% | 23% | 12% | 3% | 1% |

Women

| 22% | 25% | 28% | 17% | 7% | 1% |

n=1,374 US practicing Christian adults, June 16–July 6, 2020.

FIGURE 2.4

an important flag when it comes to helping people discover previously overlooked gifts. While anyone can struggle to identify or develop their gifts (like my son Simon), the research indicates that women may struggle with this more—a reality that all of us need to keep in mind.

Time to Reflect

What do you make of the gender discrepancy that showed up in the findings? (If you are a man, ask a woman you trust what she makes of this discrepancy as well.) What women in your life are you in a position to encourage in their gift discovery process? How could you naturally point out the gifts you notice in the women in your life?

RESEARCH INSIGHT: EACH GENERATION EXPERIENCES DISCOVERING GIFTS DIFFERENTLY

Another discrepancy in gift awareness and intentionality that showed up in the findings relates to age. While 97 percent of US practicing Christian adults believe it is at least "somewhat important" to identify and understand their gifts, practicing Christian millennials (born 1984–1998) are significantly more likely than those in older age groups to say this is "extremely important" (43% millennials versus 32%

Gen X [born 1965–1983] versus 28% boomers [born 1946–1964]).[14] This resonates with the answers given by practicing Christian millennials when asked how well they knew their own gifts, as you can see in figure 2.5.[15]

Looking at each generation's answers to this question, a more general trend seems to appear: younger generations

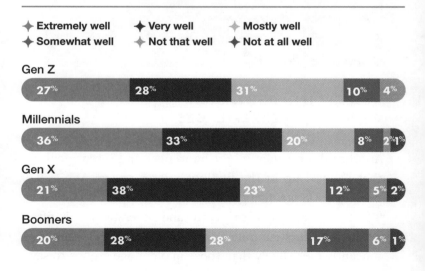

KNOWING AND UNDERSTANDING INDIVIDUAL GIFTINGS, BY GENERATION

HOW WELL WOULD YOU SAY YOU KNOW YOUR OWN GIFTINGS, ABILITIES, OR SKILLS?

Percent among practicing Christians

◆ Extremely well   ◆ Very well   ◆ Mostly well
◆ Somewhat well   ◆ Not that well   ◆ Not at all well

Gen Z
27% | 28% | 31% | 10% | 4%

Millennials
36% | 33% | 20% | 8% | 2% | 1%

Gen X
21% | 38% | 23% | 12% | 5% | 2%

Boomers
20% | 28% | 28% | 17% | 6% | 1%

n=1,374 US practicing Christian adults, June 16–July 6, 2020.

FIGURE 2.5

tend to be more likely to feel they know their gifts than older generations. Notice, in figure 2.6, practicing Christians' responses to whether they've ever taken an assessment, inventory, or test designed to help them better understand their gifts. The trend is even stronger here: the younger you are, the more likely it is that you've used a tool to help you understand your gifts.[16]

Why might younger people be more in touch with the gifts God has given them? The reasons for these discrepancies are likely complex and diverse, but their existence should raise another important flag when it comes to helping people discover previously unnoticed gifts. On the one hand, younger generations appear to be more motivated to explore their gifts—an insight church leaders and Christian mentors might want to keep in mind. On the other hand, those in older generations may need more encouragement to reflect on their many gifts.

Time to Reflect

What do you make of the generational discrepancy that showed up in the findings? (Find someone you trust who's not your age and ask them what they make of this discrepancy.) What older people in your life are you in a position to encourage in their gift discovery process?

DISCOVERING THE GIFTS GOD HAS ENTRUSTED TO US

After touring the villa in Buenos Aires, we stood with Edilberto next to the ministry center to talk details about a potential partnership later that year. Edilberto was very

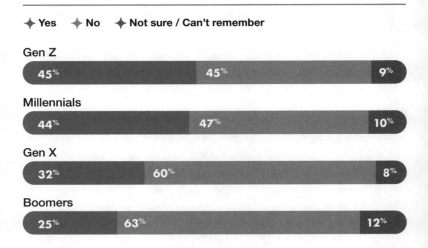

USE OF GIFTING ASSESSMENTS, INVENTORIES, OR TESTS, BY GENERATION

HAVE YOU TAKEN AN ASSESSMENT, INVENTORY, OR TEST THAT WAS DESIGNED TO HELP YOU BETTER UNDERSTAND YOUR GIFTINGS, ABILITIES, OR TALENTS?

Percent among practicing Christians

◆ Yes   ◆ No   ◆ Not sure / Can't remember

Gen Z
| 45% | 45% | 9% |

Millennials
| 44% | 47% | 10% |

Gen X
| 32% | 60% | 8% |

Boomers
| 25% | 63% | 12% |

n=1,374 US practicing Christian adults, June 16–July 6, 2020.

FIGURE 2.6

strategy minded and asked great questions about the college students who would spend three months partnering with the ministry: he wanted to know their majors, their strengths, and the particular gifts or skills they might have.

It occurred to me as we talked and planned how strong this director's focus on gifts really was. He didn't just want to know what kind of financial partnership we were proposing, he wanted to know what specific skills and abilities the students would bring. Edilberto's critical thinking, management, intercultural, and teamwork gifts were shining through.

After returning to the States we finalized the details of the partnership, and a group of college students moved into the challenging streets of that villa, spending three months using the gifts God had blessed them with to make a real difference under the leadership and guidance of Edilberto and his team.

They all did great work that summer. And I've never forgotten my day walking around with Edilberto and how quickly I focused on deficits when he first walked in the door. Like the Christians to whom James wrote his letter, I needed a paradigm shift. I needed to have my cynicism challenged. I needed to be told not to be deceived but to focus instead on "every good gift and every perfect gift" that had been given to me and those around me by a loving God. I experienced, firsthand, the power of discovering gifts. And researching how people think about their own gifts has only confirmed for me just how powerful this really can be.

May we all experience the power of discovering the gifts God has entrusted to us.

Next Steps

If you would like to tap into more of that power for yourself, here are some practical steps you could take:

OPTION 1: MEMORIZE JAMES 1:16-17.
"Do not be deceived, my beloved brothers. Every good gift and every perfect gift is from above, coming down from the Father of lights, with whom there is no variation or shadow due to change."

OPTION 2: DISCOVER YOUR GIFTS.
Discover more about your own gifts by taking the Every-Gift Inventory. The inventory will take less than twenty minutes to complete and will provide you a personalized (absolutely free) overview of where your various gifts are in twelve distinct areas and how you can be intentional about growing and sharing them going forward. Visit www.everygift.org to get started.

Once you have your results, write your top gifts in the circle.

OPTION 3: HELP OTHERS DISCOVER THEIR GIFTS.

To encourage others to discover and be attentive to the excellent gifts God has clothed and ornamented them with, make a list of five people in your life whose aptitudes, abilities, or skills you've noticed. Write their names in the circle and consider how you can point your observations out to them. You can also share the EveryGift Inventory with them and encourage them to take it. (Keep in mind that the majority of the US adults [62%] and practicing Christians [67%] who have never taken a gift assessment, inventory, or test are interesting in doing just that![16])

Only let each person lead the life
that the Lord has assigned to him,
and to which God has called him.

PAUL OF TARSUS, CIRCA AD 53
1 CORINTHIANS 7:17

To leave one's own calling and to attach
oneself to alien undertakings, surely amounts
to walking on one's ears, to veiling one's feet,
to putting a shoe on one's head, and to
turning everything upside down.

MARTIN LUTHER, CIRCA AD 1522
"GOSPEL FOR THE SUNDAY AFTER
CHRISTMAS, LUKE 2:33-40"

The doctrine of vocation encourages
attention to each individual's uniqueness,
talents, and personality. These are valued as
gifts of God, who creates and equips each
person in a different way for the calling
He has in mind for that person's life.

GENE EDWARD VEITH JR., 2002
GOD AT WORK

Everyone Is Called

THE POWER OF NAMING OUR GOD-GIVEN VOCATIONS

For roughly a thousand years during the Middle Ages, Christians had a very narrow and specific understanding of calling. If someone had a "calling" from God, this meant they were called to a religious life as a priest, a monk, or a nun. It was common knowledge all throughout the Middle Ages that those in this "spiritual estate" were the only Christians who were fully able to serve God and live a truly spiritual life. All other vocations were acknowledged as necessary but were looked down on as worldly and somewhat demeaning. The reformer Martin Luther changed all this.

As a reformer, Luther didn't just question the papacy and various unbiblical practices of the medieval church, he also questioned the church's longstanding understanding of vocation that monastic orders existed on a higher level than that of everyday Christians. Luther's biblical teaching on vocation (a word that means, literally, "calling") redefined calling for Christians around the world. Those in Luther's day began to realize, as Gene Edward Veith puts it, that "every kind of work, including what had heretofore been looked down upon—the work of peasants and craftsmen—is an occasion for priesthood, for exercising a holy service to God and to one's neighbor."[1]

Everyday Christians began to see in a new light the various roles and relationships to which they were called. For instance, when they asked God to "give us this day our daily bread," they began to understand that God often answered that prayer through the faithful labors of farmer, miller, and baker. This realization filled people with new motivation and a sense of significance in their work in home, occupation, and society, as they realized that their labors were purposeful acts of obedience and were pleasing to God. As Luther famously observed in a Christmas sermon on the shepherds who visited Jesus' manger,

> All works are the same to a Christian, no matter what they are. For these shepherds do not run away into the desert, they do not don monk's garb, they do not shave their heads, neither do they change their clothing, schedule, food, drink, nor any external

work. They returned to their place in the fields to serve God there![2]

To the church in Luther's day, this truth was as refreshing as it was exhilarating: God calls every human he creates to purposefully use their gifts to love others within the various vocations to which he has called them. Again, as Paul put it, "Having gifts that differ according to the grace given to us, let us use them" (Romans 12:6).

But how can you and I tap into the refreshing power that comes from naming our God-given vocations today? And what exactly are the practical implications of the Bible's teaching on calling?

THE LIFE GOD HAS CALLED YOU TO

First Corinthians is a letter of correction from the apostle Paul to a church that, well, needs correction. The first chapters of Paul's letter confront divisions within the church, their understanding of the gospel, sexual immorality, and lawsuits between believers, among other things.

In chapter 7, Paul addresses a long list of tricky relational issues that need to be addressed (sexual temptation, the marriage bed, singleness, widowhood, unequally yoked marriages between Christians and non-Christians). In the midst of addressing these very specific life situations, Paul gives them a more general, overarching instruction. "Only let each person lead the life that the Lord has assigned to him, and to which God has called him. This is my rule in all the churches" (1 Corinthians 7:17).

In this call to lead the life (literally in the Greek "walk in the way") that God has for them, Paul uses two significant words: *assigned* and *called*. These are "religiously freighted words" Paul has used elsewhere to speak of God *calling* people to saving faith and to refer to spiritual gifts God has *assigned* to people for ministry within the church.[3] The implications of using these two words here is noteworthy. As Keller and Alsdorf explain:

> Paul uses these same two words here when he says that every Christian should remain in the world God has "*assigned* to him, and to which God has *called* him." Yet Paul is not referring in this case to church ministries, but to common social and economic tasks— "secular jobs," we might say—and naming them God's callings and assignments. The implication is clear: just as God equips Christians for building up the body of Christ, so he also equips all people with talents and gifts for various kinds of work, for the purpose of building up the human community.[4]

Paul is inviting these Christians in Corinth to faithfully live into the different vocations or callings God has given them. This is his "rule in all the churches" and the original sense of vocation. When we hear the word *vocation* we tend to immediately think of an occupation or job, but the original sense of the word is actually all the ordinary tasks and roles of human life into which God has called us.[5]

One of the great joys of being reconciled to God through the cross is how this reconciliation paves the way to more easily discern and faithfully respond to the various vocations (roles and relationships) God has called you to in life. I got a beautiful picture of this while spending some time in northern Russia.

During my first Russian winter, I struck up a friendship with Mark, a Russian Christian who quickly became one of my heroes in the faith. As we walked around Mark's snow-laden city, he told me the story of his life: how he grew up in this very town, how he lived as a gangster doing all sorts of horrible things well into his twenties, and how, by the time he had gotten married and started to have children, these actions started to catch up to him and made him feel, in a word, *dirty*.

That's how Mark put it to me: he simply felt dirty. Then he told me the fascinating story of how, on a hiking trip, a friend shared the gospel of forgiveness with him and he came to saving faith. I'll never forget how Mark described that moment: he told me that after he confessed his sins and came to faith, he felt like "a blank sheet of paper." That part confused me, and I wondered if Mark's broken English had gone astray. But Mark assured me, when he became a Christian he felt *clean* like a blank sheet of paper: all those horrible things he'd done were gone.

Normally, that'd be the ending of a pretty cool Christian testimony, but as we walked on into the night, Mark was just getting started. He went on to tell me how, after becoming a Christian, he felt called and motivated to be a better husband and father. (Later during my visit, I got to spend time at his home with his family and was impressed by this former gangster's healthy and inviting household.)

Mark also told me he felt called to extract himself from the local gangs and use his leadership and technical gifts as a driver in a way that would benefit others. (Both weeks I was there I got to see many of his gifts used in powerful, practical ways in service to the underserved orphans in his town.)

Our walk continued, and it grew dark and began to snow more heavily. But Mark wasn't done telling me the story of his life. As we neared the center kremlin of his town, Mark took delight in telling me about his church and the ways his family was part of starting a musical drama team that shared evangelistic messages in creative ways. (I got to see one of their performances—he and all his children were involved and used their various artistic gifts.)

Finally, we arrived at the center of town, where the onion domes of the town's Orthodox Church reached higher than any other building. Mark said he wanted to show me something beautiful. I was getting pretty cold and a little confused: it was late at night, and I thought the building must be closed. But when Mark knocked on a small door, sure enough, the old door was unlocked from inside by none other than a police officer. Mark and the officer exchanged happy greetings, and the officer took us up staircase after staircase, eventually bringing us to a ladder, which led to a small opening at the dizzying height of the onion domes. There before us was the entire town.

I was struck by the beauty of Mark's town under snowfall and also by Mark's considerable connections. "How did you arrange for this?" I asked my new friend. Mark responded, "Don Donovic, I told you: this is *my* town." Mark then went on to describe the ways he had felt God calling him to use his connections among the town's gangs to reduce violence, create more jobs, and help the overall well-being of his town. Mark apparently had considerable civic gifts.

That night was memorable for many reasons. But chief among them was how adamant Mark was to tell me his whole story. It wasn't enough for me to know how he came to faith—as clean as a blank sheet of paper. He also wanted me to know what God had then written on that piece of paper—the life God had called him to. Mark's vocation (calling) in family, church, work, and society were just as central to God's work in his life as the forgiveness he had experienced while hiking with his friend.

Mark was, in essence, following Paul's rule: he was faithfully leading the life God had assigned to him and called him to. And he was being faithful to *all* the different vocations in his life. While this is an important part of every Christian's life, it also turns out this is something *all humans* are created for.

EVERYONE IS CALLED

Not only does God see everyone as a gift, and not only has God blessed everyone with gifts, but he also calls everyone he creates to use their gifts with purpose.

Although Psalm 139 lingers in the sublime moment of everyone being "fearfully and wonderfully made," it also mentions that these humans, whom God is carefully knitting together, are being made to live each day with purpose. As David writes,

Your eyes saw my unformed substance;
in your book were written, every one of them,
   the days that were formed for me,
   when as yet there was none of them.
      (Psalm 139:16)

If Psalm 139 gives a nod to the each person's days of purpose, Genesis is outright explicit. After God blesses humans in Genesis 1, bestowing on them all they need for success (*barak*), he then gives them marching orders to be fruitful and multiply and fill the earth and subdue it. A chapter later, we see more marching orders. "The LORD God took the man and put him in the garden of Eden to work it and keep it" (Genesis 2:15).

Here we see God, who created the Garden in the first place, commissioning humans as workers.[6] It is important to note that humans were called to work *prior* to the fall. Being called by God to work is, then, a part of the paradise of the Garden; it is hardwired into humanity as a basic human need. As Solomon put it, part of "God's gift to man" is that we "take pleasure in all [our] toil" (Ecclesiastes 3:12-13). This means that all humans are created for meaningful work and without it will experience "significant inner loss and emptiness."[7] As

Ben Witherington put it, "It is perfectly clear that God's good plan always included human beings working, or, more specifically, living in the constant cycle of work and rest."[8]

Since the fall, our purposeful work on earth may suffer from the curse of being made more difficult (Genesis 3), but all humans are nonetheless created as gifts with gifts to share in the work God calls them to. Work is our design and our dignity.[9] And this isn't just the case for work that employs our spiritual gifts. For example, in the pages of the Bible we see people with musical gifts called by God to use them: recall the many refrains to make music to the Lord in Psalms or the many musical instruments King David constructed for use in the temple (2 Chronicles 7:6). Or consider how God calls people to use the artistic, technical, and civic gifts he's entrusted them with: giving specific instructions to Bezalel, Oholiab, and their team of craftsmen (Exodus 36). God also empowers and instructs the labor of farmers (Isaiah 28) and underscores the importance of the actions of civic leaders (Romans 13).

Is it any surprise, then, that God not only instructs *those in his church* to "work heartily" in whatever they do (Colossians 3:23), but also calls *any who will hearken to his*

wisdom to fully embrace the work God calls them to in life? As we read in the Wisdom literature (which is a reflection on how the world works as it has been ordered for all those God has created),[10] "Whatever your hand finds to do, do it with all your might, for in the realm of the dead, where you are going, there is neither working nor planning nor knowledge nor wisdom" (Ecclesiastes 9:10 NIV).

Rather than idolizing leisure and kicking our feet against labor as some sort of unfortunate necessity for making money, the Bible's clear teaching invites us to delight in the various vocations God calls us into. In fact, the Bible's clear doctrine of vocation leads to a couple of beautiful implications in our lives.

BEAUTIFUL IMPLICATION 5: BROADENING OUR CELEBRATION OF CALLING

The good news is that everyone is called by God to use their gifts in a variety of roles and relationships. This is just as refreshing and exhilarating today as it was when Luther helped the church reclaim the doctrine of vocation five hundred years ago.

But for many Christians, a unique issue keeps us from fully embracing this news: our focus on vocations within the local church.

Obviously, the life that the Lord has assigned to each of us (to use Paul's language) does include various roles and relationships within our local church. I remember how much delight Mark took in telling me how God had called him to use his gifts at his church. Paul's image of the church as a body with diverse and varied parts (see 1 Corinthians 12) invites us to celebrate all Christians using their unique gifts in the church context.

But Mark was equally excited about how God had assigned him and called him to roles and relationships within his family, work, and society as well. This is the kind of robust understanding of vocation the Bible invites us to embrace. As Gene Edward Veith puts it,

> Vocation is a word from Latin meaning "a call." We all have a calling, in fact, many callings, through which we serve God, and we do so by serving our neighbor. And who is my neighbor? Start at home! Husband, wife, children, parent, and then move a bit further out: employers, employees, neighbors next door, down the street, in the community. Move it out further: state and nation, and the whole world.[11]

I'm reminded of a story shared by Gary Haugen, the founder of International Justice Mission (IJM). He was faithfully serving in his local church as an usher and sixth-grade Sunday school teacher when he began to wonder if there was perhaps even more God wanted to do through him (he had developed considerable leadership, technical, and civic gifts as a lawyer). Gary's wondering led him eventually to found IJM, a powerful force for fighting injustice around the world.

Gary is not only faithfully living out his vocation in the church but also in work and society, with significant results. Within twenty years of its founding, IJM had blossomed into a team of more than 750 people in offices around the world and was making powerful inroads against all manner of injustice, such as sex trafficking and child labor. Gary, like Mark, was right to embrace a robust sense of vocation in his life.

This is what the Bible's teaching on vocation can do for you: it opens your eyes to consider and wonder about the vocations God has called you to. Luther actually baked this approach into his influential *Small Catechism*. Section three of the catechism lists a "Table of Duties" under the header *"Certain Passages of Scripture for Various Holy Orders and Estates Whereby These Are Severally to Be Admonished as to Their Office and Duty."* This auspicious header is followed by Scripture applicable to various vocations including those of bishops, pastors, preachers, civil government workers, subjects, husbands, wives, parents, children, hired men, employees, employers, the young in general, and widows.

The biblical doctrine of vocation invites a broad celebration of callings like this. If you are a lawyer or teacher or
shoemaker, you can "glorify God perfectly well" by practicing law, teaching, and making shoes.[12] As Al Hsu observes, "Virtually every job or profession is indeed a good
and noble calling from God—and can reflect a divine
purpose or intent for the world."[13]

Luther went so far as to point out that if a father is
washing diapers in the home, his friends may ridicule him
"as an effeminate fool" (this was in the sixteenth century),
but "God, with all his Angels and creatures, is smiling."[14]
The reality is, work of all kinds—whether with the hands or
mind—"evidences our dignity as human beings" because it
reflects the image of our Creator God.[15]

If "no task is too small a vessel to hold the immense
dignity of work given by God,"[16] then we can "see the world
ablaze with the glory of God's work through the people he
has created and called—in everything from the simplest
actions, such as milking a cow, to the most brilliant artistic
or historic achievements."[17] This even extends to seeing
how God can be at work through our non-Christian
neighbors, who he has gifted and called as well.

My friend Mark and IJM founder Gary Haugen are re-
minders of just how beautiful and effective it can be when
Christians pay attention to all their vocations, not just
those within the church.

RESEARCH INSIGHT: PASTORS TEND TO EMPHASIZE ONE VOCATION OVER OTHERS

In spite of clear evidence in the Bible and church history that our God-given vocations extend to all areas of life, our research reveals that pastors tend to emphasize and celebrate church vocations, often to the exclusion of those outside the church. As a research team, we were curious about how Christian pastors think, talk, and teach about people's gifts and callings. As someone who has been serving as a pastor for thirteen years, I confess that the findings resonate with my own experience: we pastors spend most of our time thinking, talking, and teaching about people's vocations in one area—the local church.

While pastors tend to focus on spiritual gifts, as we've seen, when we asked them about the purpose of common gifts and how they should be used, the results were unambiguous: almost all pastors believe common gifts are "for God's glory" (95%) and "for the church's benefit" (87%). A significantly smaller percentage of pastors (68%) believe common gifts are also for the benefit of society or the local community.[18]

Perhaps not surprisingly, then, when we asked pastors about how people's gifts are celebrated, the answers varied depending on whether the gifts were being used in the church or outside the church. Eighty-two percent of pastors agreed that in their church, people's gifts are celebrated for the difference they make within the life of the church, but only 61 percent could say the same about the difference gifts are making outside the church context, as indicated in figure 3.1.[19] And 89 percent of all pastors who've taught on gifts in the last year taught specifically about "using our gifts to serve the church," while only 53 percent of pastors mentioned using gifts "for the benefit of humanity/society."[20]

Seeing these findings and reflecting soberly on my own preaching and teaching over the last thirteen years, I

GIFT CELEBRATION WITHIN THE CHURCH

PLEASE INDICATE IF YOU AGREE OR DISAGREE WITH EACH STATEMENT BELOW.

Base: US Protestant pastors

✦ **Agree strongly** ✦ **Agree somewhat** ✦ **Neither agree or disagree**
✦ **Disagree somewhat** ✦ **Disagree strongly**

People's gifts are celebrated for the difference they make *in* the church

People's gifts are celebrated for the difference they make *outside* the church

n=491 US Protestant pastors, June 23–July 28, 2020.

FIGURE 3.1

wonder what would have happened if my friend Mark had become a Christian in my church rather than his church in Russia. Might my unexamined emphasis on vocations in the church have kept him from answering God's equally important call to his family, work, and society as seriously as he did? Or what if Gary Haugen had been faithfully using his gifts at my church? Might our lack of emphasis on a robust doctrine of vocation have kept him from wondering how God might be calling him to use his gifts as a lawyer in other places?

Regardless of what our pastors do or do not teach about vocations, these findings are a wake-up call for all of us to lift up our eyes and consider how to lead the life God has assigned to us and called us to in our families, our work, and our society—at least as much as we consider doing the same in the church.

Reflection and Discussion

Reflecting back over the last year, what have you heard or read about your gifts and God's invitation to use those gifts with purpose? What do you find most appealing and compelling about a broad, robust understanding of vocation?

BEAUTIFUL IMPLICATION 6: INFUSING EVERYDAY LIFE WITH A SENSE OF PURPOSE

The good news that everyone is called not only challenges more narrow views of calling but also has a way of infusing everyday life with a sense of purpose. This is part of what was so refreshing and invigorating for Christians in Luther's day and has the promise to do the same for us today.

If the only purpose for our daily strivings in our work is to gain money (and, presumably, the leisure and comfort money can secure for us), we are left with a thin, materialistic, self-centered organizing principle for our everyday lives. This is deeply dissatisfying for humans, who were fearfully and wonderfully made, clothed and ornamented with gifts, and called by God to use those gifts with purpose in this world. As Gene Edward Veith observes:

> People sin in their vocations, and they sin against their vocations. And in not being aware of what their vocations are—and that there is a spiritual dimension to work, family, and involvement in society—they are plagued by a lack of purpose, confused as to what they should do and how they should live and who they are.[21]

Without a sense of vocation we can be left wondering what the point of all our struggles and efforts and daily sacrifices and faithfulness really add up to. Is there some direction or purpose or meaning for our lives? *Call* and *vocation* are categories the Christian tradition has long used to address such issues.[22] As William C. Placher put it in his history of twenty centuries of Christian wisdom on vocation,

> If the God who made us has figured out something we are supposed to do, however—something that fits how we were made, so that doing it will enable us to glorify God, serve others, and be most richly ourselves—then life stops seeming so empty: my story has meaning as part of a larger story ultimately shaped by God.[23]

It is transformative to realize there is something (or some-*things*) that God has called you to do with your life. Hugh Whelchel experienced this personally and writes about it in his book *How Then Should We Work? Rediscovering the Biblical Doctrine of Work*, "Discovering the Biblical doctrine of work transformed my life. Work for me went from being just a means to an end, to having transcendent purpose in and of itself."[24]

The importance of this sense of purpose is underscored in a sobering way when you consider those who are, for some reason, prevented from using their gifts in everyday faithfulness. My friend Dan has dedicated his leadership and critical thinking gifts to helping gifted but overlooked people find employment. Again and again, Dan has witnessed how those who are not working struggle with their self-worth and sense of purpose and dignity. And he's seen how life changing it can be to labor purposefully with your gifts.

Dan told me of a refugee who had languished for years in a refugee camp in central Africa, but he became infused with hope and purpose and joy when he finally got to use his God-given gifts to labor with purpose. The experience was so profound for this man that it even had a spiritual impact on his life. As he testified to Dan, "I feel like I'm the only one God knows about!" It's just not enough to have your basic needs provided for; we are all created as gifts with gifts to share, and when we use them, we find meaning and purpose.

APPLYING GIFTS

"I FEEL I AM ABLE TO MAKE GOOD USE OF—OR APPLY—MY GIFTINGS."

Base: those who know and understand their gifts well

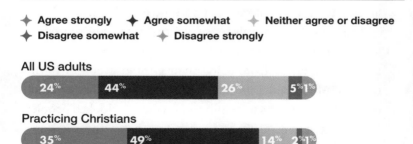

◆ Agree strongly ◆ Agree somewhat ◆ Neither agree or disagree
◆ Disagree somewhat ◆ Disagree strongly

All US adults

| 24% | 44% | 26% | 5% | 1% |

Practicing Christians

| 35% | 49% | 14% | 2% | 1% |

n=1,391 US adults who know and understand their gifts well, June 16–July 6, 2020.
n=1,305 US practicing Christian adults who know and understand their gifts well, June 16–July 6, 2020.

FIGURE 3.2

Paul's rule for all the churches seems simple enough, doesn't it? "Only let each person lead the life that the Lord has assigned to him, and to which God has called him" (1 Corinthians 7:17). How powerful it is when we actually do that!

RESEARCH INSIGHT: CHRISTIANS EMBRACE USING THEIR GIFTS WITH PURPOSE

Interestingly, our research shows that Christians are a bit more likely than the average US adult to feel they are making good use of their gifts. As you can see in figure 3.2, many US adults (68%) and an overwhelming majority of practicing Christians (83%) agree that they feel they are able to make good use of their giftings.[25]

Little variance showed up when we broke down the answers to this question by generation, gender, education, and socioeconomic status.[26] What exactly does this mean? It seems to suggest that despite one's identity or background, what plays a larger role in making use of one's gifts is whether they are a practicing Christian.

Is it possible that the Bible's teachings on vocation have put Christians in a better position to feel they can make good use of their various gifts? The research doesn't indicate this specifically, but it does tell us that practicing Christians are much more likely than all US adults to say that their gifts, abilities, and talents come from God (fig. 3.3).[27] This is perhaps an indication of the ways practicing Christians think about their gifts and their call to use them.

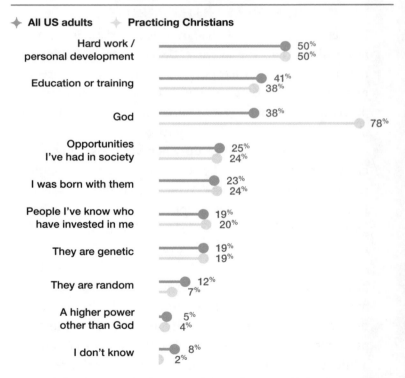

ORIGIN OF GIFTINGS

WHERE DO YOUR OWN GIFTINGS, ABILITIES, AND TALENTS COME FROM?

Base: those who know and understand their gifts well

✦ **All US adults** ✦ **Practicing Christians**

	All US adults	Practicing Christians
Hard work / personal development	50%	50%
Education or training	41%	38%
God	38%	78%
Opportunities I've had in society	25%	24%
I was born with them	23%	24%
People I've know who have invested in me	19%	20%
They are genetic	19%	19%
They are random	12%	7%
A higher power other than God	5%	4%
I don't know	8%	2%

n=1,391 US adults who know and understand their gifts well, June 16–July 6, 2020.

n=1,305 US practicing Christian adults who know and understand their gifts well, June 16–July 6, 2(

FIGURE 3.3

> ## Time to Reflect
>
> Using the possible answers in figure 3.2, how much do you agree or disagree with this statement: "I feel I am able to make good use of—or apply—my giftings"?
>
> Using the possible answers in figure 3.3, where would you say your gifts, abilities, and talents come from? How might you have answered these questions differently five or ten years ago?

NAMING OUR GOD-GIVEN VOCATIONS

Back in Russia, Mark and I stayed for a while at that overlook in one of the ancient onion domes towering over his town. Our conversation eventually died down, and we watched the falling snow in silence.

I'm not sure what Mark was thinking about as he looked out at his hometown, but my mind was filled with the rich testimony he had just spent the evening sharing with me. That image he shared to describe his conversion, "like a blank sheet of paper," lingered in my mind, as did the stories of how his new life in Jesus infused passion, direction, and purpose in his daily life at home, in church, at work, and in the greater society of his hometown.

Eventually we climbed back down to the ground level. I thanked Mark for the unforgettable evening, and we parted ways as he headed back toward his parked car and I toward my hotel.

I took my time on that walk, partly to enjoy the beautiful snowfall and partly to linger on everything I had heard that night. It felt like a holy sort of night, when God could get through to even a stubborn disciple like me. I've never forgotten Mark's living testimony of finding purpose and meaning by simply using his God-given gifts in the vocations God has assigned to him. (It didn't hurt that my roommate was already snoring when I got back to the room—I had ample opportunity to pray and reflect that night!)

Mark's story inspired me to reengage with certain vocations (as son, brother, and neighbor) that I had been mostly ignoring. This experience, combined with the time spent considering research findings and exploring the doctrine of vocation, has convinced me of the power of naming the vocations God has given us.

May we all experience this power more fully in our lives.

Next Steps

If you would like to tap into more of this power for yourself, here are some practical steps you could take:

OPTION 1: MEMORIZE ONE OF THESE BIBLE VERSES.

"Only let each person lead the life that the Lord has assigned to him, and to which God has called him.

This is my rule in all the churches" (1 Corinthians 7:17).

"Whatever you do, work heartily, as for the Lord and not for men, knowing that from the Lord you will receive the inheritance as your reward. You are serving the Lord Christ" (Colossians 3:23-24).

OPTION 2: CREATE A VOCATIONAL MAP.
Creating a vocational map can help you name the various vocations God has called you to in your own life. For each realm of life (family, church, work, society) list the different roles and relationships God has assigned to you. Spend time reflecting on your vocations and praying for God's help in faithfully leading the life God has for you.

As iron sharpens iron,

so one person sharpens another.

KING SOLOMON, CIRCA 940 BC
PROVERBS 27:17 NIV

I said to him, my dear Mentor, why did

I refuse to follow your Counsels?

FRANÇOIS FÉNELON, 1699
THE ADVENTURES OF TELEMACHUS,
THE SON OF ULYSSES

We all have a stewardship

responsibility to continue to develop

what God has given us.

PAUL STANLEY AND ROBERT CLINTON, 1992
CONNECTING

Everyone Can Grow

THE POWER OF HELPING EACH OTHER GROW IN OUR GIFTS

While most of us have never read the French novel *Les Aventures de Télémaque* written by François Fénelon in 1699, it has nonetheless affected how you and I think and talk about helping each other grow. Fénelon (a theologian, poet, and writer) penned this novel while he was serving as the tutor to the young Duke of Burgundy. The novel is set within the story of Homer's *Odyssey* and focuses on Telemachus's educational travels, accompanied by his own wise tutor named Mentor. Ultimately, it is a story about the importance and beauty of one person helping another person develop and grow.

Fénelon's novel was an immediate bestseller and became one of the most-read books of its time. People were immediately attracted to the rich portrayal of Mentor's influence (one person helping another grow), and the book was quickly translated into many languages. It is to this popularity and influence that we can attribute our English word for helping each other grow: *mentoring*.

The universally popular appeal of the concept of mentoring is a sign that there's something about pursuing growth and development that is wired into us as humans. As we'll discuss, the Bible points to the fact that God expects every human to grow, develop, and mature over time—including growth in how we share our gifts in our various vocations.

But how can you and I embrace growth and an overall developmental posture as a normal part of our lives? And what exactly does growing in our gifts have to do with God and the church?

AS IRON SHARPENS IRON

While Fénelon's novel may have popularized the concept and ideal of people helping each other grow, there was nothing actually novel about the concept itself. Two and a half millennia earlier, King Solomon gave the world this memorable image, "As iron sharpens iron, so one person sharpens another" (Proverbs 27:17 NIV). Humans help each other grow.

In fact, one of the key themes of the book of Proverbs is that wise people seek after growth, instruction, and correction, while fools avoid all three. This theme is stated in the orienting introduction to the book of Proverbs:

> Let the wise hear and increase in learning,
> and the one who understands obtain guidance. . . .
> Fools despise wisdom and instruction.
> (Proverbs 1:5, 7)

Wise people seek after growth and development. Fools despise it. This seeking is meant to be active: later in Proverbs we are encouraged to "call out" for insight and raise our voices for understanding. In fact, we are told to search for instruction as we would search for silver or for hidden treasures (Proverbs 2:3-4).

This search is so beautiful to behold that it makes you think we were actually made to be pushed to grow and to push others toward growth. At times the pushing goes just one way (as in classic mentoring relationships), but it's common for there to be mutual pushing. I saw a beautiful picture of this under my own roof during the early quarantine months of 2020.

As the initial shelter-in-place orders were put in place in March 2020, my oldest, Simon, came home to finish his sophomore year of college from our basement. And my middle child, Teya, experienced her last semester of high school in a much different way than she had always imagined she would. With Wendy and me also asked to work remotely from home and Victor shifting to remote middle school, our meager square footage and Wi-Fi capacity were both pushed to their limits.

In the midst of that uncomfortable, unwelcomed season of difficult circumstances, Simon and Teya did an unexpected thing together: they started a small business. You would've had to witness the previous years of their sibling relationship to appreciate just how shocking and beautiful it was to see them partnering together. With Simon's entrepreneurial gifts and Teya's artistic gifts they birthed a Christian clothing brand called Adriel Collective.[1]

I just loved the "business meetings" Simon and Teya would schedule and hold. It was not difficult to overhear these meetings (small square footage, remember?). It was beautiful to hear Teya helping Simon grow his entrepreneurial gifts and Simon helping Teya develop her artistic gifts. Whether brainstorming a concept for a new line of shirts, critiquing one of Teya's original designs, or working out kinks on Simon's website and e-commerce solutions, Simon and Teya were graciously but clearly pushing on each other's gifts. They asked each other to grow and learn new skills; they gave honest feedback. They were like iron sharpening iron.

I don't know what was more impressive to behold (and overhear) as a parent: their fast-paced growth as entrepreneur and artist, or the honest push and pull they engaged in. The growth and instruction and correction happening in that season is what Proverbs would happily deem *wisdom* and rightly celebrate. And all this from a brother and sister separated by only sixteen months in age.

Being crammed into the same house for a few months turned out to be a time of celebrating each other's gifts and pushing each other to grow in those gifts. Simon and Teya were being wise. Their lives were a reflection of Solomon's unforgettable image: people sharpening each other as iron sharpens iron. This is an important nuance of the Bible's anthropology: these wonderfully made humans who are using their God-given gifts in various vocations are meant to be constantly developing their aptitudes, abilities, and skills.

EVERYONE CAN GROW

It's not only Wisdom literature that explicitly calls people to seek diligently after instruction and correction. We also see example after example of purposeful, iron-sharpening-iron relationships all throughout the Bible. At times these relationships are focused on developing character or faithfulness; other times they are focused on developing skills and abilities. As Walter Brueggemann points out, people helping each other grow in the Bible "moves back and forth between an acute theological sensibility and quite practical awareness of specific tasks that need to be accomplished."[2] We see examples of such relationships throughout the Old Testament, including

Jethro and Moses,
Moses and Joshua,
Eli and Samuel,
David and Solomon,
Elijah and Elisha,
Huldah and Josiah,
Naomi and Ruth, and
Mordecai and Esther.

These relationships, and others, are narrated in such a way that they clearly celebrate the act of people helping each other grow and develop. Again and again, these relationships result in a blessed sharpening of skills and abilities or character and faithfulness.

We see the same types of relationships in the New Testament. Jesus, of course, was interested in more than just helping people grow, but it is striking that his overall ministry of healing and teaching included a more intimate, unhurried development of his twelve disciples. And isn't it noteworthy that Luke tells us that Jesus himself "increased in wisdom and in stature" (Luke 2:52)?

We also see iron-sharpening-iron relationships between Barnabas and Paul, and between Paul and many others. In the New Testament, we see that developmental relationships are central to the mission of the church going forward. Is it any wonder, then, that Paul encourages all believers to be like iron to each other? "Therefore encourage one another and build one another up, just as you are doing" (1 Thessalonians 5:11).

From cover to cover, the Bible celebrates humans helping each other grow. If we really started seeking after instruction and correction like people searching for hidden treasure, this would likely have two beautiful implications: a normalizing and celebration of this developmental posture, and a reigniting of gift development within the church.

BEAUTIFUL IMPLICATION 7: CELEBRATING A DEVELOPMENTAL POSTURE

The fact that God designed us to pursue growth does not mean we always embrace growth. While it may be true that helping each other grow "is as old as civilization itself,"[3] it is equally true that *resisting* growth is as old as civilization itself. It may be foolish to resist instruction and correction, as Proverbs clarifies, but at times it is mighty tempting to do just that. Why? Well, a developmental posture "is not inevitably congratulatory, but also includes correction and perhaps reproof."[4]

So we, at times, resist growth because we don't want the pain that can accompany correction and reproof. This is a theme in Fénelon's novel, as Telemachus confesses at one point: "This Counsel was useful and honourable, but I had not Prudence enough to follow it, and heark'ned only to my own Passion; yet the wise Mentor lov'd me to such a degree, that he condescended to accompany me in that Voyage, which I rashly undertook against his Advice."[5]

I can relate to Telemachus: I don't always embrace and celebrate a developmental posture like my children did during the quarantine. For example, midway through my first season in ministry, I asked Kevin, an elder at my church in Boulder, Colorado, to help me grow in my preaching gifts. I was initially excited at the prospect—I had never received anything other than compliments on my preaching and was excited to be pushed and sharpened. I asked Kevin specifically because of his critical thinking gifts and because he was the most well-read person in theology and church history I had ever met—specific technical gifts that were especially relevant. I was excited when Kevin agreed to help me.

But I soon found out that growing is a humbling, sometimes painful, process. Week after week, I read books on preaching that Kevin gave me (starting with those by the Puritans). These books challenged my core assumptions of what a sermon even was, let alone how to prepare and deliver one.

That growth process was humbling and almost embarrassing at times. Our conversations were frustrating and confusing and exhilarating and captivating, all at the same time. I found Kevin's counsel to be "useful and honorable," to use Telemachus's words. And I am so glad that God gave me the gift of that season. Those hours spent being pushed and enlightened, encouraged and prayed for, sharpened and corrected are hours I look back on fondly in spite of the pain involved.

So whenever I feel God calling me into a new season of developing my skills, I remember that time with Kevin and try to shrug off my hesitation. I have to keep choosing to embrace a developmental posture in life. And this isn't just me. Every person has to continue to embrace being developed, challenged, and sharpened.

Sadly, after reflecting on research into the lives of six hundred past and present leaders, Paul Stanley and Robert Clinton observed, "Most people cease learning by the age of forty. By that we mean they no longer actively pursue knowledge, understanding, and experience that will enhance their capacity to grow and contribute to others. Most simply rest on what they already know."[6]

In their research, Stanley and Clinton observed five characteristics of people who "finish well" in life; two of them relate directly to embracing a developmental posture. People who finish well

- maintain a positive learning attitude all their lives, and

- have a network of meaningful relationships and several important mentors during their lifetime.[7]

Stanley and Clinton, both Christians, lament that so many people are tempted to plateau and "become satisfied with where they are and what they know," a posture that they see as clearly contradicting the biblical principle of stewardship—continuing to develop what God has given us.[8]

God calls all of us to seek after growth and development, not to despise it. We're supposed to search for learning and correction as we would search after hidden treasures. That's what it looks like to be good stewards of the aptitudes, abilities, and skills God has entrusted to us. We should celebrate this developmental posture.

RESEARCH INSIGHT: PEOPLE ARE HUNGRY TO GROW THEIR GIFTS

Chasing after growth seems to be something people both inside and outside the church are looking for. In our research, we wanted to explore how hungry or hesitant people are to develop their various gifts and found out that about four in ten US adults (40%) and practicing Christians (37%) agree that their skills are not developed enough.[9]

Recognizing that your skills are not sufficiently developed is one thing, but wanting to develop specific skills is quite another. And when we asked people if they have a gifting, ability, or skill they would "really like to develop," 39 percent of practicing Christians and 34 percent of the general population answered "definitely."[10] Given the large percentages of people who answered "maybe," there are really only a minority of people who outright said they didn't really want to develop a gift (fig. 4.2).

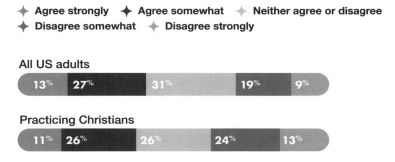

DOUBT SURROUNDING GIFTEDNESS
"MY SKILLS AREN'T DEVELOPED ENOUGH."

✦ **Agree strongly**   ✦ **Agree somewhat**   ✦ **Neither agree or disagree**
✦ **Disagree somewhat**   ✦ **Disagree strongly**

All US adults

| 13% | 27% | 31% | 19% | 9% |

Practicing Christians

| 11% | 26% | 26% | 24% | 13% |

n=1,504 US adults, June 16–July 6, 2020.
n=1,374 US practicing Christian adults, June 16–July 6, 2020.

FIGURE 4.1

Time to Reflect

Do you personally agree or disagree with the statement: "My skills aren't developed enough"? How would you characterize your current hunger for growing your gifts?

RESEARCH INSIGHT: SOME PEOPLE ARE ESPECIALLY HUNGRY TO GROW IN THEIR GIFTS

Some fascinating trends appeared when we analyzed how interested in developing their gifts different groups of people are. For example, when you isolate for those who are more aware of their gifts and compare their answers

DESIRE FOR DEVELOPING GIFTS

ARE THERE GIFTINGS, ABILITIES, OR SKILLS
YOU WOULD REALLY LIKE TO DEVELOP?

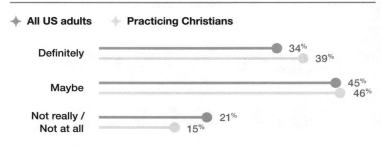

◆ **All US adults**   ◆ **Practicing Christians**

Definitely — 34% 39%

Maybe — 45% 46%

Not really / Not at all — 21% 15%

n=1,305 US adults, June 16–July 6, 2020.
n=1,374 US practicing Christian adults, June 16–July 6, 2020.

FIGURE 4.2

with those who are not aware of their gifts, a pretty clear correlation becomes evident (see fig. 4.3).[11]

These findings underscore an important dynamic between discovering gifts and growing gifts. They also wave a flag: people who don't have high awareness of their gifts may need more encouragement to pursue growth and development.

Another fascinating trend appeared when we broke down people's answers to this question based on generation. In general, those in younger generations are much more likely to say they have giftings, abilities, and skills they would really like to grow. As you can see in figure 4.4, when asked, "Are there giftings, abilities, or skills you would

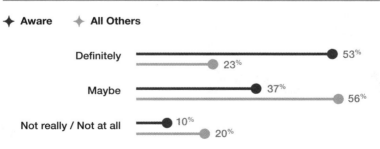

PRACTICING CHRISTIANS' INTEREST IN DEVELOPING GIFTS

ARE THERE GIFTINGS, ABILITIES, OR SKILLS YOU WOULD REALLY LIKE TO DEVELOP?

◆ Aware   ◆ All Others

	Aware	All Others
Definitely	53%	23%
Maybe	37%	56%
Not really / Not at all	10%	20%

n=1,504 US adults, June 16–July 6, 2020.
n=1,374 US practicing Christian adults, June 16–July 6, 2020.

FIGURE 4.3

really like to develop?" 69 percent of practicing Christians in Gen Z answered "definitely"—which is much higher than the average for practicing Christians in general (39%). Fifty-six percent of millennials answered the same, and the numbers keep dropping from there: only 46 percent of Gen X and a thin 21 percent of boomers definitely have gifts they'd really like to develop.[12]

PRACTICING CHRISTIANS' INTEREST IN DEVELOPING THEIR GIFTS, BY GENERATION

ARE THERE GIFTINGS, ABILITIES, OR SKILLS YOU WOULD REALLY LIKE TO DEVELOP?

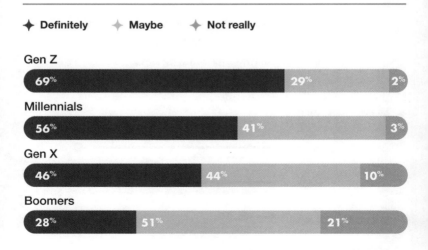

✦ Definitely   ✦ Maybe   ✦ Not really

Gen Z
69% | 29% | 2%

Millennials
56% | 41% | 3%

Gen X
46% | 44% | 10%

Boomers
28% | 51% | 21%

n=1,374 US practicing Christian adults, June 16–July 6, 2020.

FIGURE 4.4

These generational findings underscore two distinct realities. First, it seems that younger people are hungry to grow their gifts, abilities, and skills. This is a helpful insight for all those who are working with (or parenting!) those in younger generations.

On the other hand, those in older generations appear to be less in touch with this desire to grow gifts. For some, this could be due to the fact that they are already well-developed experts in their craft and are more focused on helping those

DOUBT SURROUNDING GIFTEDNESS

"AS I'VE AGED, I HAVE GROWN OUT OF TOUCH WITH MY GIFTINGS AND SKILLS."

✦ **Agree strongly** ✦ **Agree somewhat** ✦ **Neither agree or disagree**
✦ **Disagree somewhat** ✦ **Disagree strongly**

All US adults

Practicing Christians

n=1,504 US adults, June 16–July 6, 2020.
n=1,374 US practicing Christian adults, June 16–July 6, 2020.

FIGURE 4.5

of the next generation grow. For others, this could be a sign of the "settling" dynamic Stanley and Clinton have observed in their research. And it's possible that some have simply grown out of touch with their gifts, a dynamic we specifically asked about (fig. 4.5).[13] One in three US adults (33%) agree that they have grown out of touch with their giftings and skills.

Time to Reflect

How would you answer the question, "Are there giftings, abilities, or skills you would like to develop?" (definitely, maybe, or not really/not at all)? How does your answer match up with the overall answers of others in your generation?

BEAUTIFUL IMPLICATION 8: REIGNITING GIFT DEVELOPMENT WITHIN THE CHURCH

This good news—that God expects us to faithfully steward our gifts by developing them over time—can help reignite gift development within the church. Historically this has happened, whether formally or informally, through relationships.

This relational aspect of helping each other grow is what Fénelon so compellingly illustrated in his novel: Mentor was journeying through life with Telemachus, helping him develop and grow along the way. Mentoring like this has been the primary way of passing on knowledge and skills in every field and in every culture throughout human history.[14] How do you learn a trade, skill, or practice? By apprenticing yourself under someone who has already developed the same gift.

Only in recent decades has the universal reliance on this kind of relationship-based gift development begun to shift to a reliance on "computers, classrooms, books, and videos."[15] This has made relational gift development a little less common in our culture. I have noticed this same shift in many of our churches: while classes and programs are almost always present in a church, the same cannot be said about iron-sharpening-iron relationships. As a result, many Christians have been missing out on the riches of helping each other grow.

My experience of being developed in preaching with Kevin's help was painful at times, yes, but it was rich and rewarding and encouraging as well. And it better prepared me to use the communication gifts God has entrusted to me. This is why I haven't hesitated to do the same thing for others with communication gifts, specifically gifts in teaching. For example, my good friends and partners in my church, Andy, Mary, and AmyRuth, all have clearly been entrusted with gifts in teaching. Because of that, I have not only invited them to use those gifts within the church but also offered to help them develop those gifts.

What a joy it has been to dedicate time specifically to helping them grow and develop their considerable gifts in teaching! These iron-sharpening-iron relationships make perfect sense within the church: we acknowledge that our gifts are entrusted to us by God, we are committed to using these gifts where God calls us, and we have a context of grace in which to push for growth.

The great thing is that gift development can often go both ways. While I may have been the more experienced and trained teacher, there were many times when Andy's leadership gifts (developed over years of experience as a firefighter), Mary's technical gifts (from years working with parents and children), and AmyRuth's interpersonal gifts (honed during years of counseling practice) gave them each insights and instincts that helped me sharpen my own teaching as well. This kind of relational gift development is beautiful, rich, and rewarding.

RESEARCH INSIGHT: THE CHURCH IS A GREAT PLACE FOR GROWING GIFTS

As our research reveals in several findings, the church is an ideal place for investing in gift development.

First, we were curious about various benefits that come with developing your gifts. We asked people to respond to this statement: "As I grow in my gifts, I find that I also grow in my closeness to God." Remarkably, we found that 97 percent of all practicing Christians and 82 percent of all US adults agreed with this statement (fig. 4.6).[16]

Think of the implications of this: the vast majority of *everyone* in our country feels closer to God when they grow in their gifts. Whether a church is passionate about discipleship or evangelism or both, our findings reveal that helping people grow and develop their gifts is a strategically fruitful endeavor. And the relationships in which

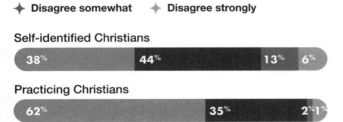

GROWING IN GIFTINGS AND CLOSENESS TO GOD

"AS I GROW IN MY GIFTS, I FIND THAT I ALSO GROW IN MY CLOSENESS TO GOD."

✦ **Agree strongly**   ✦ **Agree somewhat**
✦ **Disagree somewhat**   ✦ **Disagree strongly**

Self-identified Christians

| 38% | 44% | 13% | 6% |

Practicing Christians

| 62% | 35% | 2% | 1% |

n=980 US adults who self-identify as Christian, June 16–July 6, 2020.
n=1,374 practicing Christian adults, June 16–July 6, 2020.

FIGURE 4.6

those gifts are developed are likely to bear fruit in areas well beyond gift development.

Second, our research shows that slightly more practicing Christians (60%) compared with all US adults (52%) have previously invested in helping someone else develop their gifts (fig. 4.7).[17] It would appear that Christians are a bit more experienced in the kind of iron-sharpening-iron relationships we are discussing.

Third, it turns out there is a decent level of openness (including among non-Christians) to developing gifts in a church context. As figure 4.8 shows, there are a variety of places where people would be interested in developing their gifts, including with a small group of friends, online, or at

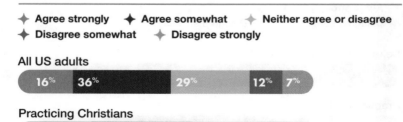

HELPING OTHERS DEVELOP THEIR OWN GIFTS

"I HAVE INVESTED IN HELPING SOMEONE ELSE DEVELOP THEIR GIFTINGS."

✦ Agree strongly   ✦ Agree somewhat   ✦ Neither agree or disagree
✦ Disagree somewhat   ✦ Disagree strongly

All US adults

| 16% | 36% | 29% | 12% | 7% |

Practicing Christians

| 23% | 37% | 24% | 11% | 5% |

n=1,504 US adults, June 16–July 6, 2020.
n=1,374 US practicing Christian adults, June 16–July 6, 2020.

FIGURE 4.7

work. But notice that practicing Christians would prefer to develop their gifts at church more than any other place. A surprising one in five US adults (who attended church at least once in the last year) also indicated church as a place they would most be interested in developing their gifts.[18]

AREAS FOR GIFT DEVELOPMENT

WHERE OR WITH WHOM WOULD YOU BE MOST INTERESTED IN GROWING, DEVELOPING, OR INVESTING IN YOUR GIFTINGS, ABILITIES, OR SKILLS? SELECT ALL THAT APPLY.

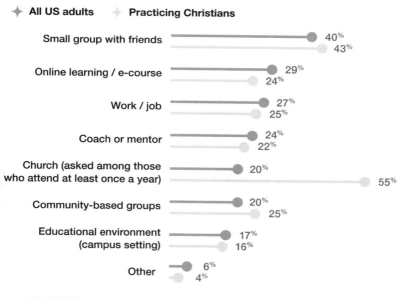

◆ All US adults   ◆ Practicing Christians

Small group with friends — 40% / 43%

Online learning / e-course — 29% / 24%

Work / job — 27% / 25%

Coach or mentor — 24% / 22%

Church (asked among those who attend at least once a year) — 20% / 55%

Community-based groups — 20% / 25%

Educational environment (campus setting) — 17% / 16%

Other — 6% / 4%

n=1,208 US adults who are interested in developing their giftings, June 16–July 6, 2020.
n=1,208 US practicing Christian adults who are interested in developing their giftings, June 16–July 6, 2020.

FIGURE 4.8

Fourth, our research reveals some troubling disparities in gift development that ought to matter to churches. As the researchers summarized,

> Practicing Christian men are more likely than women to say someone has set aside time to help them develop their gifts (68% vs. 52%). . . . As can be expected, those with a higher level of education are more likely to say someone has invested in helping them develop their gifts (52% high school or less, 61% some college or technical school, 70% college graduate or higher), a trend that also rings true along socioeconomic lines (42% lower socioeconomic status vs. 72% higher socioeconomic status). [19]

If there is any place that could and *should* step into this gap and promote opportunities for all people (regardless of gender, education, or socioeconomic status) to invest in their gifts, it is the church. Especially when you consider that the majority of those who have *not* already put effort into developing their gifts have never been offered an opportunity to do so.[20]

Time to Reflect

Which of the four findings do you feel points most compellingly to the church as a great place for gift development?

PEOPLE WHO INVEST IN THE DEVELOPMENT OF OTHERS' GIFTINGS

WHO HAS INVESTED IN THE DEVELOPMENT OF YOUR GIFTINGS, ABILITIES, OR TALENTS?

Base: those who have been invested in

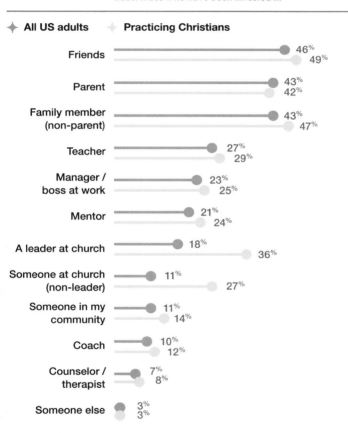

◆ **All US adults**   ◆ **Practicing Christians**

	All US adults	Practicing Christians
Friends	46%	49%
Parent	43%	42%
Family member (non-parent)	43%	47%
Teacher	27%	29%
Manager / boss at work	23%	25%
Mentor	21%	24%
A leader at church	18%	36%
Someone at church (non-leader)	11%	27%
Someone in my community	11%	14%
Coach	10%	12%
Counselor / therapist	7%	8%
Someone else	3%	3%

n=733 US adults who have been invested in, June 16–July 6, 2020.

n=868 practicing US Christian adults who have been invested in, June 16 -July 6, 2020.

FIGURE 4.9

RESEARCH INSIGHT: CHURCHES COULD INVEST MORE IN GIFT DEVELOPMENT

Our research shows that people are hungry to grow in their gifts, they are open to doing that at church, and when people grow in their gifts they grow closer to God. It would seem the opportunity for gift development in the church is substantial.

Our findings reveal, however, that our churches are not currently embracing and promoting gift development as they could. Notice in figure 4.9 that only about a third of practicing Christians report that a leader in their church has invested in developing their gifts (36%) and even fewer report someone else at their church doing the same (27%).[21] It would seem that iron-sharpening-iron relationships such as those I had with Kevin, Andy, Mary, and AmyRuth are not as common within the church as they could be.

Even in those churches that *are* teaching about gifts, "mentorships and nurturing of gifts" is one of the topics that is addressed *the least* (fig. 4.10).[22]

Time to Reflect

Who has invested in the development of your giftings, abilities, or skills? What have you heard taught about gifts in your own church over the last couple years?

TOPICS OF GIFTEDNESS TEACHINGS IN THE CHURCH

WHAT DID YOU (OR ANOTHER LEADER) TEACH OR DISCUSS WITH REGARD TO GIFTINGS? SELECT ALL THAT APPLY.

Base: pastors who say their church has taught on giftings

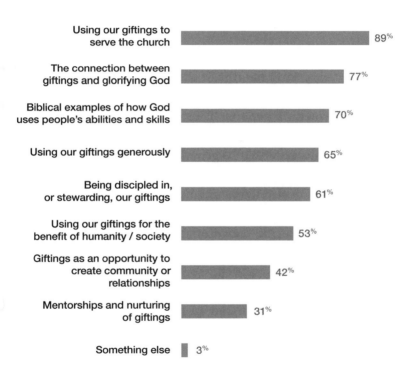

Using our giftings to serve the church — 89%

The connection between giftings and glorifying God — 77%

Biblical examples of how God uses people's abilities and skills — 70%

Using our giftings generously — 65%

Being discipled in, or stewarding, our giftings — 61%

Using our giftings for the benefit of humanity / society — 53%

Giftings as an opportunity to create community or relationships — 42%

Mentorships and nurturing of giftings — 31%

Something else — 3%

n=289 US Protestant pastors whose churches have taught on giftings within the past year, June 23–July 28, 2020.

FIGURE 4.10

While the church may not be as active as it could be in helping people in the development of their God-given gifts, the good news is that the church is a great place for this to happen, and it is beautiful to behold and experience when it does.

HELPING EACH OTHER GROW OUR GIFTS

Back in those early months of the quarantine, our home became a laboratory not only for the Adriel Collective but also for growth in general. There was lots of iron sharpening iron. Not only did we get to overhear Simon and Teya pushing each other to grow and develop as an entrepreneur and an artist Simon also took it upon himself to push my youngest, Victor, and me to get into shape.

You see, Simon was doing a fair amount of physical training with Marine recruiters at the time, and suffice it to say, the Marines are fairly adept at helping each other grow in physical fitness. While the Marines tend to stick to fairly structured hierarchies of authority, outside the military we can all be like iron sharpening iron. We can all help each other. Apparently, Simon believed this firmly as he expressed his desire to help not only his younger brother to grow in physical fitness, but also me, his dad.

Victor was a gracious and willing participant, I must say. I, on the other hand, would joke about grounding Simon as he put me through intricate group workouts in the basement, runs around the neighborhood, and weight-lifting until it hurt. *Who told Simon*, I thought, *that he could just push me to grow like this?* I ran, did pushups and planks, and generally allowed myself to be pushed, cajoled, and cheered to get into shape.

And here's the thing, even though that experience was painful (let the reader understand), it was also beautiful and joyful and thoroughly human. We are wired to be like iron sharpening iron, to be open to helping each other grow in all sorts of ways—including in developing the gifts God has given us. And the research findings we've discussed only confirmed this and convinced me of just how important it is to help each other grow.

May we all experience the power of helping each other grow in our gifts.

Next Steps

If you would like to tap into more of that power for yourself, here are some practical steps you could take:

OPTION 1: MEMORIZE ONE OR TWO OF THESE PASSAGES:

> As iron sharpens iron, so one person sharpens another. (Proverbs 27:17 NIV)

> Therefore encourage one another and build one another up, just as you are doing.
> (1 Thessalonians 5:11)

> Let the wise hear and increase in learning,
>   and the one who understands obtain guidance,
> to understand a proverb and a saying,
>   the words of the wise and their riddles.

> The fear of the LORD is the beginning of knowledge;
>   fools despise wisdom and instruction.
>   (Proverbs 1:5-7)

OPTION 2: CHOOSE A GIFT TO DEVELOP.

Go back to your EveryGift results (from chapter two) and choose one of the gifts you wanted to develop. Write the gift you want to develop in the left box, then write the name of someone who can help you develop that gift in the middle box. Finally, consider which realm you are most interested (or feel most called by God) to use your developing gift for. Make contact with the person you listed and ask them if they would help you craft a development plan together.

My gift I want to develop:

Someone who can help me develop my gift:

My gift will help my: *(circle one)*

Family   Church

Work   Society

OPTION 3: LEARN MORE ABOUT GIFT DEVELOPMENT.
Read and work through *Discover Your Gifts Workbook: Twelve Sessions for Exploring Your God-Given Purpose.* This practical workbook is based on our research findings and is designed to help you discover, share, and grow your own gifts, as well as to equip you to help others in your life do the same thing.

And he gave the apostles, the prophets,
the evangelists, the shepherds and teachers,
to equip the saints for the work of ministry.

PAUL OF TARSUS, CIRCA AD 61
EPHESIANS 4:11-12

Do not live entirely isolated,
having retreated into yourselves, as if you
were already [fully] justified, but gather instead
to seek together the common good.

BARNABAS, CIRCA AD 100
EPISTLE OF BARNABAS

When God's church is thriving,
his people are getting what they
need to be used by him in this world.

TOM PFIZENMAIER, 2012
AS QUOTED IN GO *AND DO*

Every Church Can Equip

THE POWER OF UNLEASHING PEOPLE TO USE THEIR GIFTS

How has God made you and everyone you know? He has made each of us a gift with gifts to share. And he calls every one of us to grow those gifts and share them in a variety of vocations. As we've unpacked these hopeful truths, we've explored implications for the local church. But now it's time for us to ask the question straight on: What is the role of the local church when it comes to all these gifts?

For starters, let's recognize that God's people have always been on a mission. From the moment God told Abram to *go* from his homeland (to become a nation that would bless all the families of the earth) to the moment

Jesus told his disciples to *go* from Jerusalem (to bring good news to the ends of the earth), it has been clear that God's people are sent to the world around them. We are sent to proclaim God's good news in word and deed.

Yet the Christian church has struggled with a huddling instinct from the beginning. To use Jesus' metaphor: the church has always been tempted to hide their light under a basket rather than put it on a stand. This is why church leaders have been committed from the beginning to constantly unleash the members of their churches, reminding them of their mission and nudging them out the door to engage in that mission.

This is what Barnabas, an early church leader (probably not the Barnabas mentioned in the New Testament), was getting at in his letter when he encouraged those in his church to not "live entirely isolated, having retreated into yourselves," but to instead "seek together the common good."[1] Barnabas was urging Christians to embrace their mission, not shy away from it.

Church leaders like Barnabas have always been called not to just feed and care for those in the church but also to "equip the saints for the work of ministry," as Paul put it (Ephesians 4:12). Jesus called his church to be a blessing to the world and instructed its leaders to unleash *everyone* in the church to labor together toward that end.

But how can today's church be reenergized to unleash people in this way? And in what ways could this affect each church's relationship with its surrounding community?

EQUIP THE SAINTS

There is a power in the church that we are tempted to underestimate. Consider the first churches in Asia Minor to whom Paul wrote a circular letter. They were in a period of difficulty, facing persecution from the Roman Empire and from their pagan neighbors. In such moments it is tempting to view the church as a victim—and perhaps a small, unarmed victim at that.

But Paul knew differently. As we see in Ephesians, when he looked at the young churches in Asia Minor, he saw saints who had been blessed with every spiritual blessing (Ephesians 1:3). He saw adopted sons and daughters (Ephesians 1:5) who had been created for good works that were prepared specifically for them to do (Ephesians 2:10). In Ephesians, Paul lifts the eyes of the believers to look not just at their enemies—the various "powers" arrayed against them (Ephesians 6:12)—but also at what God had done for them and what God could do through them.

It is a powerful, encouraging letter. It reminded everyone in those churches that they had power for the mission God had called them to. And it reminded church leaders to use their own gifts for a very important task. As Paul wrote,

"He gave the apostles, the prophets, the evangelists, the shepherds and teachers, to equip the saints for the work of ministry" (Ephesians 4:11-12).

Paul is saying that God has generously given variously gifted leaders to the church for a purpose: to equip everyone else in the church.

Some of us may be tempted to think that church leaders are the ones to do the work and the rest of us cheer them on (and pay them). But Paul is saying something different: church leaders are the ones to equip *everyone else* to do the work. This is the only way, Paul goes on to reason, the church will grow up to maturity—when "each part is working" (Ephesians 4:16).

As a pastor, I can be tempted to focus only on the leadership tasks that Paul himself engaged in and pay too little attention to the actual "work of ministry" for which he wanted to unleash all the saints. This bias of mine was confronted and unseated when I attended Hutchmoot a couple of years ago.

Hutchmoot is a Christian conference focused on inspiring, equipping, and unleashing Christian artists, musicians, writers, and craftsmen of all sorts to use the unique gifts God has entrusted to them. I have been to dozens (if not hundreds) of Christian conferences for leaders over the years, but as Hutchmoot began, I realized that I had never been to a conference that was not focused on leaders.

As I attended plenary sessions, read the conference materials, shared meals with others, and attended breakout sessions, I began to become conscious of these leadership-centric blinders I had been wearing unconsciously. I realized I had been looking at the church and myself and the world through a pair of lenses that had a certain tint to them (namely, leadership is all that matters). Ironically, leadership isn't even my top gift! How refreshing it was to be inspired, equipped, and unleashed as a writer, artist, and communicator during Hutchmoot.

It's not that leadership isn't supremely important in and for the church, of course. God has generously given leaders to the church, after all. But for what purpose? So that everyone in the church will be inspired, equipped, and unleashed to use their gifts in the actual work for which God has gifted and called them.

Part of what was so refreshing about Hutchmoot was how the breakout sessions were varied and practical. For someone who was used to conference breakout sessions all being about leadership in some manner or fashion, it was jarring to see breakouts focused on such labors as songwriting, gardening, guitar building, midwifery, and reading out loud.

There really should be nothing surprising about investing in unleashing *all* the saints to use *all* their gifts to bless others. It turns out this is the vision throughout the Bible: God's people are on a mission of blessing. And that mission necessitates releasing everyone in the church (including gardeners, luthiers, and midwives) to take part in it.

EVERY CHURCH CAN EQUIP

God's people, whether constituted as a nation (in the Old Testament) or as a church (in the New Testament), have always been on a mission. God's people are meant to be caught up in God's work in the world.

This is true whether God is working as Creator (helping people experience more of the shalom they were created for) or as Redeemer (reconciling all things to himself through Jesus). Whatever God is doing, his people are to be caught up in that work. We see this right at the moment God initiates Israel as his people,

> Now the LORD said to Abram, "Go from your country and your kindred and your father's house to the land that I will show you. And I will make of you a great nation, and I will bless you and make your name great, so that you will be a blessing. . . . And in you all the families of the earth shall be blessed." (Genesis 12:1-3)

From this moment forward we know that God is "committed to the mission of blessing the nations through the agency of the people of Abraham."[2] This includes God's people being "bearers of shalom" in all aspects of life,[3] as well as announcing to all people "the universal reign of God through Christ."[4]

This call to be a blessing in word and deed is not negated during tough times. There's never a time for God's people to circle the wagons and forget the world around them. In exile in Babylon, for example, God was very clear about this,

> Thus says the LORD of hosts, the God of Israel, to all the exiles whom I have sent into exile from Jerusalem to Babylon: Build houses and live in them; plant gardens and eat their produce. . . . But seek the welfare of the city where I have sent you into exile, and pray to the LORD on its behalf, for in its welfare you will find your welfare. (Jeremiah 29:4-5, 7)

Even in exile, when it would have been justifiable for God's people to be defensive against or isolated from the people and community around them, God calls his people "to be faithfully present within it."[5] That faithful presence included using all of the gifts God had entrusted to them— you need gifts to build houses and plant gardens and seek the welfare of an entire city, after all.

The same is true for God's people in the church. Paul is clear in Ephesians that those in the church are God's workmanship, created for good works (Ephesians 2:10). Even when facing opposition from "the powers" (Ephesians 6:12), God's people are called to love their neighbors, give witness to the gospel, and pursue the common good—all activities that require the use of the aptitudes, abilities, and skills God entrusted to them.

Which explains why Paul sees "equipping the saints" as a central job for church leaders. If God's people are to use their agency in service to God's work of spreading shalom and good news, they need to be equipped and unleashed for that work.

If our local churches had the same kind of focus on unleashing people with all sorts of gifts as I observed at Hutchmoot, we would see two beautiful implications in our churches: churches would be energized to unleash the gifts of the congregation, and we would reengage with our surrounding communities in exciting ways.

BEAUTIFUL IMPLICATION 9: ENERGIZING LOCAL CHURCHES TO UNLEASH THE GIFTS OF THE CONGREGATION

Paul's call for church leaders to equip the saints for ministry tells us that a local church is thriving when its members "are getting what they need to be used by God in this world."[6]

This isn't as simple as asking for volunteers or having a sign-up list, of course. Churches are filled with "a multitude of wildly disparate people with a variety of personalities, gifts, and callings."[7] It takes purposeful effort to equip each person to discover their gifts, grow in those gifts, and share them in the various vocations God has given them. Equipping doesn't just happen. It requires the steady work of a church's leaders.

My friend Matthew experienced this kind of church leadership when he became a Christian in London in his early thirties. The expectation in his church was that God was going to "get you doing something." Even as a young Christian, Matthew's gifts were celebrated, and he was encouraged by leaders in the church to use them. Matthew was a filmmaker and was encouraged to use his technical and artistic gifts in service to God's purposes in the church and in the world.

Matthew told me that his pastor, John (who used his leadership, teamwork, interpersonal, and entrepreneurial gifts to equip others for ministry), was always pointing out gifts people had and inviting them to use those gifts. Pastor John had a saying he repeated again and again: "Church is a place where everyone gets to play." As

Matthew confessed, this focus on unleashing everyone "was on the messy side from time to time," but as a result everyone at Matthew's church saw themselves and their gifts as a part of what God was doing in the world.

Matthew's church in London and the Hutchmoot conference have something in common: they are an "outpost of sorts, a launching pad for ministry and service to the world."[8]

As a pastor I really believe that "God not only saves and grows and nurtures Christians, he also invites us to get caught up with what he is doing in the world."[9] And I believe I am called as a church leader to equip the saints for ministry. I really do. But I have to admit that my leadership in the church does not always reflect these beliefs. If I'm honest, I spend a whole lot of my time doing ministry for the saints. Or to them.

This, of course, is a huge temptation for church leaders: to only see the congregation as an audience or students or clients, and only see ourselves as performers or teachers or caregivers. This approach to leadership may be cleaner and neater and more gratifying in some ways, but it ignores the fact that God has given people like me (apostles, pastors, evangelists, shepherds, and teachers) to the

WHERE GIFTINGS ARE MOST COMMONLY NOTICED BY OTHERS

WHERE ARE (OR WERE) YOUR GIFTINGS MOST COMMONLY NOTICED BY OTHERS? SELECT ALL THAT APPLY.

Base: those who know and understand their gifts well

◆ **All US adults**   ◆ **Practicing Christians**

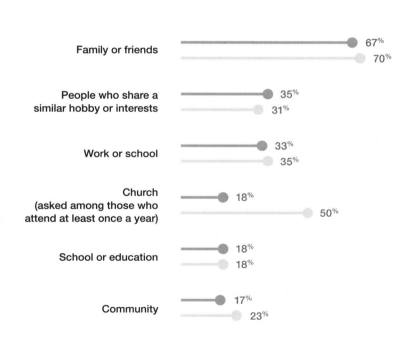

Family or friends — 67%, 70%

People who share a similar hobby or interests — 35%, 31%

Work or school — 33%, 35%

Church (asked among those who attend at least once a year) — 18%, 50%

School or education — 18%, 18%

Community — 17%, 23%

n=1,391 US adults who know and understand their gifts well, June 16–July 6, 2020.
n=1,305 US practicing Christian adults who know and understand their gifts well,
   June 16–July 6, 2020.

FIGURE 5.1

church for a singular reason: to unleash the saints to use their gifts in a variety of vocations. This is what Amy Sherman calls vocational stewardship and, as she has observed, when church leaders unleash the gifts of the congregation in this way, "congregants experience newfound joy, meaning and intimacy with Christ."[10]

Hearing the good news that every church can equip emboldens me and clarifies my calling. It makes me want to be more like Pastor John in London and the organizers of Hutchmoot. Biblical clarity on this matter can do the same for all churches: energize us for unleashing the gifts of those in the congregation.

RESEARCH INSIGHT: THE CHURCH IS IDEALLY POSITIONED TO UNLEASH PEOPLE'S GIFTS

Our research indicates that the church is well-positioned to unleash people's gifts. When we asked those who identified having at least three gifts where their gifts are most often noticed by others, the church came up quite a bit. As figure 5.1 shows, 50 percent of practicing Christians have had their gifts noticed at church—more than any other location except among "family and friends."[11]

So people are somewhat accustomed to having their gifts noticed at church. Even among all US adults who've attended church at least once in the last year, almost one in five (18%) report having their gifts noticed in church.

SETTINGS IN WHICH GIFTING ASSESSMENTS, INVENTORIES, OR TESTS ARE TAKEN

IN WHAT SETTING(S) HAVE YOU TAKEN AN ASSESSMENT, INVENTORY, OR TEST THAT WAS DESIGNED TO HELP YOU UNDERSTAND YOUR GIFTINGS, ABILITIES, OR TALENTS?

Base: have taken an assessment

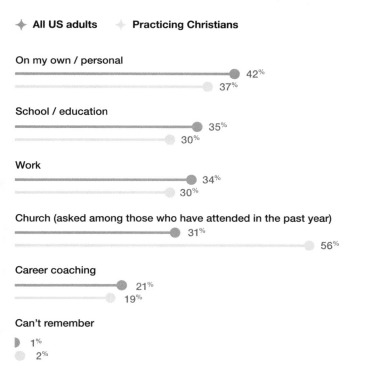

✦ **All US adults**　　✦ **Practicing Christians**

On my own / personal
42%
37%

School / education
35%
30%

Work
34%
30%

Church (asked among those who have attended in the past year)
31%
56%

Career coaching
21%
19%

Can't remember
1%
2%

n=350 US adults who have taken a gifting assessment, June 16–July 6, 2020.
n=476 US practicing Christian adults who have taken a gifting assessment, June 16–July 6, 2020.

FIGURE 5.2

When you ask those who have taken a gift assessment where they took that assessment, it turns out that over half of practicing Christians (56%) and almost a third (31%) of all US adults who attended church at least once in the last year report having taken a gift assessment at church. For practicing Christians, this was actually the most common place to take a gift assessment, as you can see in figure 5.2.[12]

But what about those who've never taken a gift assessment? Many of those surveyed who have never taken a gift assessment expressed interest in doing so (62% of all US adults and 67% of practicing Christians who have never taken an assessment expressed interest—fig. 5.3).[13]

For many of those who are interested in developing their gifts, there is a real openness to doing that in a church context, as we've already noted. In light of this, it's not too surprising to learn that over three-quarters of pastors report that helping people discover, grow, and share their gifts is an important priority in their church.[14] The church really is ideally positioned to unleash people's gifts.

Time to Reflect

Using the answers in figure 5.1, where would you say your gifts are most commonly noticed by others? How have you seen discovering, growing, or sharing gifts prioritized in your church?

RESEARCH INSIGHT: CHURCHES HAVE AN OPPORTUNITY TO GET BETTER AT UNLEASHING

While there is much in the findings to be encouraged about, some sober realities are evident. As the researchers noted,

> Church leadership has a distinct opportunity here—and, at this point, a missed one. Adults both inside and outside the Church are willing to take assessments to help identify and better understand their unique skills

POTENTIAL INTEREST IN GIFTING ASSESSMENTS, INVENTORIES, OR TESTS

HOW INTERESTED WOULD YOU BE IN TAKING AN ASSESSMENT, INVENTORY, OR TEST THAT CAN HELP YOU BETTER UNDERSTAND YOUR GIFTINGS, ABILITIES, OR TALENTS?

Base: have not taken an assessment

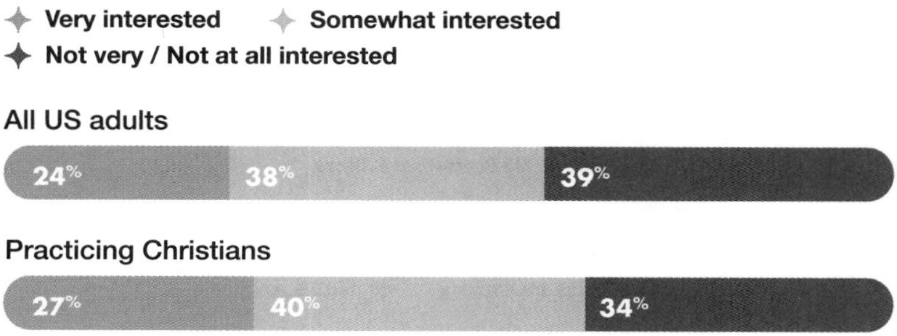

✦ **Very interested**   ✦ **Somewhat interested**
✦ **Not very / Not at all interested**

All US adults

| 24% | 38% | 39% |

Practicing Christians

| 27% | 40% | 34% |

n=1,154 US adults who have not taken a gifting assessment, June 16–July 6, 2020.
n=898 US practicing Christian adults who have not taken a gifting assessment, June 16–July 6, 2020.

FIGURE 5.3

and abilities. This is a ripe area for personal and vocational discipleship, and perhaps even a chance for outreach to non-Christians, younger adults and other community members who are in seasons of exploring their giftedness. Most pastors and their churches, however, are not tapping into this openness—either because they don't offer such assessments at all (45%) or because they only provide them to some people (31%).[15]

In other words, we have room to grow. As we've already seen, only one in three practicing Christians say one of their church leaders helped develop their gifts. And less than a quarter of all pastors (23%) say their church uses a gifts inventory for everyone in the church (fig. 5.4). Forty-five percent report not using a gifts inventory at all.[16]

USE OF GIFTING ASSESSMENTS IN THE CHURCH

DOES YOUR CHURCH TAKE A "GIFTS INVENTORY" (A SURVEY OF SKILLS, TALENTS, OR RESOURCES) OF ITS MEMBERS OR ATTENDERS?

Base: US Protestant Pastors

◆ **Yes, for everyone**   ◆ **Yes, just for some people**
◆ **No, we do not take a gifts inventory**   ◆ **Not sure**

| 23% | 31% | 45% | 1% |

n=491 US Protestant pastors, June 23–July 28, 2020.

FIGURE 5.4

Of course, inventories aren't the only way to help people discover their gifts. As you can see in figure 5.5, the most common method (reported by 88% of pastors) is having a pastor get to know members of the church personally, or having lay leaders do the same (reported by 53% of pastors).[17]

While there is much to recommend a personal, relational approach like this, the research suggests that the results might not always be sufficient. We asked pastors how much they agree or disagree with the statement, "As a pastor, I feel I have a good sense of the giftings of our congregation." Only 16 percent agreed strongly with this statement—far fewer than those who agreed strongly that they know people's occupations (fig. 5.6).[18] It turns out Matthew's pastor, John, is a bit of an outlier, unfortunately.

The reality is almost half (48%) of all pastors admit that their church's efforts to identify people's giftings is not very structured, and another 16 percent say it's not structured at all. How many pastors report having a very structured approach to helping people discover their gifts? Only 5 percent.[19] As Amy Sherman notes, "There are very few churches that have strong, intentional systems for deploying their people's time and their talent."[20]

In short, our research reveals that churches have a real opportunity in front of them: a chance to get better at unleashing everyone's gifts.

IDENTIFYING GIFTS WITHIN
THE CONGREGATION

HOW DOES YOUR CHURCH LEARN ABOUT OR IDENTIFY THE GIFTINGS IN YOUR CONGREGATION? SELECT ALL THAT APPLY.

Base: US Protestant pastors

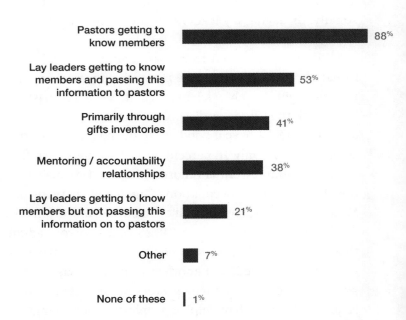

Pastors getting to know members	88%
Lay leaders getting to know members and passing this information to pastors	53%
Primarily through gifts inventories	41%
Mentoring / accountability relationships	38%
Lay leaders getting to know members but not passing this information on to pastors	21%
Other	7%
None of these	1%

n=491 US Protestant pastors, June 23–July 28, 2020.

FIGURE 5.5

Time to Reflect

How good a sense do you think your church leaders have of the gifts in the congregation? How are people in your church most commonly helped to discover and develop their gifts?

BEAUTIFUL IMPLICATION 10: REENGAGING LOCAL CHURCHES WITH THEIR SURROUNDING COMMUNITIES

This good news, that every church can equip, inevitably leads churches to reengage with their surrounding communities.

Many Christians and churches have perhaps unintentionally isolated themselves from their surrounding

HOW PASTORS VIEW GIFTEDNESS WITHIN THEIR CHURCH

✦ **Agree strongly** ✦ **Agree somewhat** ✦ Neither agree or disagree
✦ **Disagree somewhat** ✦ **Disagree strongly**

As a pastor, I feel I have a good sense of the giftings in our congregation.

16%   64%   12%   8%

I know most people's occupation in our congregation.

50%   38%   6% 5% 1%

n=491 US Protestant pastors, June 23–July 28, 2020.

FIGURE 5.6

neighborhoods and communities. The huddling instinct has lulled the church from the very beginning—there was a reason Barnabas had to urge Christians to be careful to not "live entirely isolated, having retreated into yourselves."

We at Lutheran Hour Ministries have noticed this huddling instinct in a previous study exploring how Christians are (or are not) relating with their neighborhoods. The findings were ultimately very hopeful but also underscored how isolated some Christians and churches have become from their surrounding communities (for more of our findings, see *The Hopeful Neighborhood*[21]).

Our research on neighborhoods ultimately led us to launch a nationwide network, The Hopeful Neighborhood Project, to encourage people (including Christians and churches) to reengage with their surrounding neighborhoods and communities. It has been simultaneously hopeful to walk with people as they begin to pay attention to their neighborhoods for the first time and sobering to see what a dramatic paradigm shift this is for so many.

While the church may be tempted to isolate itself, God uses his Word to continually call his people to engage with the people and places right around them. As Jesus put it in the Sermon on the Mount, "In the same way, let your light shine before others, so that they may see your good

works and give glory to your Father who is in heaven"
(Matthew 5:16).

We Christians aren't supposed to put our light under a
basket but to let others see it—a reality that presumes we
are engaged with the people and places around us. By
helping Christians discover, grow, and share their gifts,
churches will be helping more Christians participate not
just in the life of the church but also in the life of their
families, workplaces, and communities. This could pave the
way for us to move away from a sort of "civic privatism"
toward a different and better way to engage the world.[22]

Not only can equipping churches unleash congregants
to engage with the world around them, they can also reengage with their communities in a unique way by becoming a welcoming place for non-Christians who want
to discover and develop their gifts too. In my own church
I've seen non-Christian musicians come into the church
to grow and share their musical gifts as part of a worship
team. I've also seen non-Christian actors cross the
threshold of a church for the first time just for the
chance to work with the drama team and gifted director
in our congregation.

As our research has shown, many people (not just Christians) are hungry to discover and develop their gifts.
Equipping churches can become places for those within or
outside the faith to discover, grow, and share their gifts.

RESEARCH INSIGHT: LOCAL CHURCHES ARE
PRIMARILY FOCUSED ON THE LOCAL CHURCH

Some particular obstacles and opportunities need to be kept in mind for those who want to develop an equipping church. As someone who has served as a pastor for over thirteen years, I can attest to the sober reality that most churches wind up focused on what their pastor focuses on—and often that winds up being the local church. As Dr. Davida Crabtree observed, "The church exists for the mission, for the sake of the world. Yet it is organized to build itself up as an organization. It blesses the work its members do within the institution but pays no attention to the work they do 'outside' the church."[23]

Pastors are more likely to view people's gifts as being for the glory of God (95%) and the church's benefit (87%) than for the benefit of society (68%) or the local community (68%).[24] When churches use gift inventories to help people discover their gifts, they are most often using them "to connect people with opportunities to serve in the church."[25] This focus on gifts used inside the church is clear, too, when you look at what churches are teaching about gifts. As figure 5.7 highlights, the most common teaching in churches that teach about gifts is about "using our giftings to serve the Church."[26]

The local church needs to reckon with this tendency to emphasize its own needs.

TOPICS OF GIFTEDNESS TEACHINGS IN THE CHURCH

WHAT DID YOU (OR ANOTHER LEADER) TEACH OR DISCUSS WITH REGARD TO GIFTINGS? SELECT ALL THAT APPLY.

Base: pastors who say their church has taught on giftings

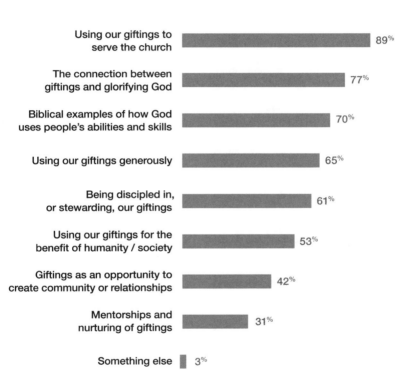

- Using our giftings to serve the church — 89%
- The connection between giftings and glorifying God — 77%
- Biblical examples of how God uses people's abilities and skills — 70%
- Using our giftings generously — 65%
- Being discipled in, or stewarding, our giftings — 61%
- Using our giftings for the benefit of humanity / society — 53%
- Giftings as an opportunity to create community or relationships — 42%
- Mentorships and nurturing of giftings — 31%
- Something else — 3%

n=289 US Protestant pastors whose churches have taught on giftings within the past year, June 23–July 28, 2020.

FIGURE 5.7

WHO GIFTINGS ARE INTENDED FOR

WHO ARE YOUR OWN GIFTINGS, TALENTS, AND ABILITIES FOR?

Base: those who know and understand their gifts well

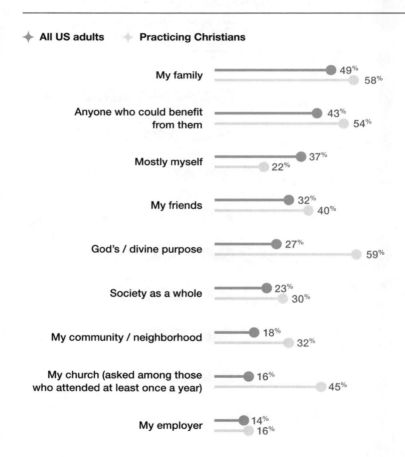

◆ **All US adults**   ◇ **Practicing Christians**

My family — 49% / 58%

Anyone who could benefit from them — 43% / 54%

Mostly myself — 37% / 22%

My friends — 32% / 40%

God's / divine purpose — 27% / 59%

Society as a whole — 23% / 30%

My community / neighborhood — 18% / 32%

My church (asked among those who attended at least once a year) — 16% / 45%

My employer — 14% / 16%

n=1,391 US adults who know and understand their gifts well, June 16–July 6, 2020.
n=1,305 US practicing Christian adults who know and understand their gifts well,
    June 16–July 6, 2020.

FIGURE 5.8

Time to Reflect

Why do you think there is a bias toward focusing on what our gifts can do inside our churches instead of out in the community?

RESEARCH INSIGHT: CHRISTIANS ARE POISED TO USE THEIR GIFTS FOR THEIR COMMUNITY

While pastors and churches tend to emphasize gifts being used within the church, this is not necessarily the case with individual Christians.

We asked people who they think their gifts are for. While almost half of all practicing Christians answered "my church" (45%), even more answered "God's/divine purpose" (59%), "my family" (58%), and "anyone who could benefit from them" (54%). On the whole, practicing Christians have a fairly wide sense of why God has entrusted them with gifts.

Our findings also suggest Christians are more primed than the average US adult to use their gifts in their local community. For example, we asked people if they have a sense of "belonging" to their community. We asked this question because social cohesion theory tells us that people who have a sense of belonging to their community are much more likely to be active in pursuing the common good there. Although churches and Christians are tempted to isolate themselves, we found that practicing Christians are quite a bit more likely to have a sense of belonging in their community than all US adults. As you can see in figure 5.9, 70 percent of practicing Christians have this important sense of belonging, whereas only 49 percent of all US adults reflect a sense of belonging to their community.[27]

When we asked people if they have any experience in carrying out a project for the benefit of others in their community, we discovered that 38 percent of practicing Christians but only 29 percent of all US adults have done so.[28] In addition, we wanted to gauge future interest, so we asked people, "How interested would you be in working with people in your neighborhood, using each person's giftings

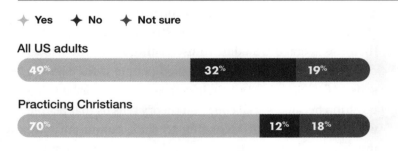

HAVING A SENSE OF BELONGING

WOULD YOU SAY YOU HAVE A SENSE OF "BELONGING" TO YOUR COMMUNITY?

✦ Yes   ✦ No   ✦ Not sure

All US adults

| 49% | 32% | 19% |

Practicing Christians

| 70% | 12% | 18% |

n=1,504 US adults, June 16–July 6, 2020.
n=1,374 US practicing Christian adults, June 16–July 6, 2020.

FIGURE 5.9

and skills, to carry out a project with others in your community?" Again, practicing Christians were slightly more likely to be very or somewhat interested (71%) than all US adults (60%), as you can see in figure 5.10.[29]

These findings indicate that, on the whole, Christians are poised to use their gifts for their communities. These findings line up with what we experienced after launching The Hopeful Neighborhood Project. While this network is explicitly designed for people of any faith or no faith, we have seen Christians in particular jump at the chance to gather a group of

INVESTING INDIVIDUAL GIFTINGS IN THE LOCAL COMMUNITY

HOW INTERESTED WOULD YOU BE IN WORKING WITH PEOPLE IN YOUR NEIGHBORHOOD, USING EACH PERSON'S GIFTINGS AND SKILLS, TO CARRY OUT A PROJECT FOR THE BENEFIT OF OTHERS IN YOUR COMMUNITY?

✦ **Very interested**   ✦ **Somewhat interested**   ✦ **Not very interested**
✦ **Not at all interested**   ✦ **Not applicable**

All US adults

| 18% | 42% | 23% | 15% | 1% |

Practicing Christians

| 27% | 44% | 19% | 8% | 2% |

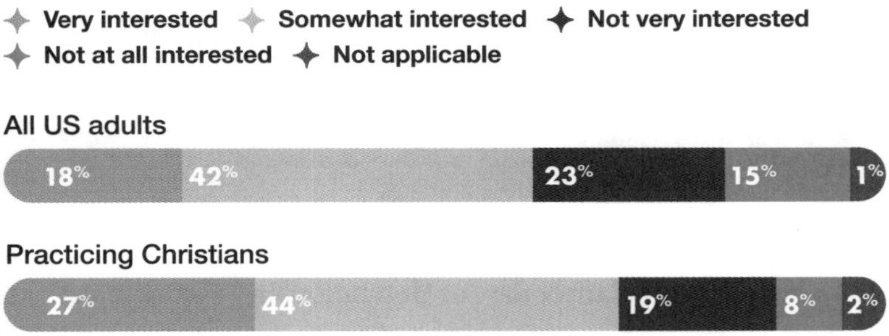

n=1,504 US adults, June 16–July 6, 2020.
n=1,374 US practicing Christian adults, June 16–July 6, 2020.

FIGURE 5.10

neighbors to use their gifts for good in the neighborhood. From day one, the phones of our neighborhood coaches started ringing. Neighborhood coach Sara put it this way:

> As I connect with faith leaders all over the globe . . . from a small rural congregation in Rogue River, Oregon to a bustling and dense neighborhood in central Honduras, I have a deep sense that God is stirring hearts toward authentic collaboration and connection among neighbors as they pursue the common good together.

Our research indicates that Christians are poised for the kind of hopeful collaboration and connection Sara mentions.

Time to Reflect

Using the options given in figure 5.8, how would you answer the question: "Who are your own giftings, talents, and abilities for?" How would you answer the question posed in figure 5.10? Do you feel your interest level has changed over time?

UNLEASHING PEOPLE TO USE THEIR GIFTS

I walked through all three days at Hutchmoot in a sort of joyful haze. I listened to the conference chef read original essays he'd written about and for the occasion of each dinner. I watched three visual artists collaboratively create art together while discussing the role of community in art-making. I ate handmade jam that one "Mooter" had brought, spread over a slice of bread baked in the home of another gifted Mooter.

On Saturday morning, I happened upon a long line of tables crowded with all manner of handmade items. I found an awesome brown cloth bag that I thought would be great for carrying books back and forth from the library. But when I went to buy it, I was confused: there were no price tags.

Looking around, I noticed a sign above the tables that cleared up my confusion. Apparently, these tables were for graciously giving and gratefully receiving handmade items. Gifts are for giving and receiving, the sign declared.

I walked away from the line of tables with that awesome brown bag and with the distinct impression that where people are unleashed to use their God-given gifts, a spirit of generosity naturally blossoms.

The rest of the weekend I breathed in this generosity and thought about how much more interesting and fruitful and fun life is when people of all sorts are un-leashed to be generous with the gifts God has given them. That's something we're made for, I think. That experience, along with what we've learned about people and their gifts, makes me long for churches everywhere to embrace equipping the saints for the work God calls them to.

May we all experience the power of unleashing people to use their gifts.

Next Steps

If you would like to tap into more of this power for yourself, here are some practical steps you could take:

OPTION 1: MEMORIZE ONE OF THESE VERSES FROM EPHESIANS.

"And he gave the apostles, the prophets, the evangelists, the shepherds and teachers, to equip the saints for the work of ministry" (Ephesians 4:11-12).

"For we are his workmanship, created in Christ Jesus for good works, which God prepared beforehand, that we should walk in them" (Ephesians 2:10).

OPTION 2: HELP UNLEASH GIFTS IN YOUR CHURCH.
Explore the suite of practical resources rooted in our research and strategically designed to help churches become more purposeful in unleashing gifts. You can discover more about these resources at www.lhm.org/gifted and then consider ways these tools could help your small group or church unleash the gifts God has given you.

OPTION 3: HELP UNLEASH GIFTS IN YOUR NEIGHBORHOOD.
Learn more about how you and your neighbors could use your gifts to make a difference in your neighborhood by checking out The Hopeful Neighborhood Project or contacting a neighborhood coach at hopeful neighborhood.org.

Conclusion

BUZZ'S CONCERT

A few years after Mom and Buzz moved in with us, we collectively developed an idea: What if we held a concert for Buzz at our church? Buzz was something of a pianist, you see. In spite of his lingering mobility issues stemming from a severe car accident in his twenties, Buzz had taught himself, over the years, to play the piano with two thumbs and a couple fingers.

He wrote his own songs (mostly about Jesus) and loved to play and sing when he had the energy and occasion. His songs were as quirky as you would imagine they would be, and playing wore him out physically. But there was just something about those rare moments when Buzz was playing and singing for others. It just made you smile. In those moments it was clear to all that Buzz was a gift with gifts to share.

I think that's why we landed on the idea of a concert. It felt important to us and to Buzz that he share his gifts. Now, ours is a large suburban church. Would it surprise you to hear that most Sundays Buzz was the only one with tattoos and studded suspenders? He kind of stuck out, and most folks didn't really know what to make of him. I could tell many of them looked at him as I had at first: they saw only his deficits.

So for Buzz's sake and for our sakes, and maybe even for the sake of our church, we planned Buzz's Concert. We reserved the chapel, inviting friends and folks who'd met Buzz. We set up lots of chairs and positioned the piano and microphone. On the day of the concert, Buzz was a little nervous. I think we all were. How many people would show up? Would Buzz's pain flare up? What would happen when we put him in front of a microphone?

I tell you, it was a great concert.

An awkward start, sure: I finished my emcee introduction, the packed crowd cheered . . . and Buzz just looked at me. "Do I start now, Donnie?"

"Yes, Buzz. It's all you!"

"So, what do I do? What do I play?" I just smiled up at Buzz and shrugged. "Just share your songs, Buzz. Share your gift." And he did. It was a great concert.

One of my children was recording the whole thing on my phone, including the laughter and applause and the long line of well-wishers coming up to shake Buzz's hand afterward. I still watch that shaky video from time to time. Even with the awkward framing and out-of-focus moments and poor sound quality, the message of that concert comes through loud and clear: Buzz is a gift with gifts to share. And God called him to use those gifts.

God has since called Buzz home to heaven. I imagine Buzz is holding lots of concerts now.

But I'm convinced that we don't have to wait until heaven to see ourselves and everyone we know in the way God sees us: carefully crafted masterpieces that he has fearfully and wonderfully knit together.

When we focus on deficits in ourselves and in others, we inevitably get stingy and annoyed and a little mean. But when we focus on discovering every gift and return to our first-article truths, a more hopeful path is opened up to us. It is possible for us to look at each other as we looked at Buzz during that glorious concert: as gifts with gifts to share.

MAKER OF ALL THINGS VISIBLE AND INVISIBLE

It's easy enough to recite the first article of the Apostles' Creed (*We believe in God, the Father Almighty, Maker of heaven and earth*), but it's something else entirely to then pause and consider, biblically and practically, what exactly this means.

When we follow Luther's lead, we realize just how much important truth is pointed out in this first article. As we've explored, the Bible not only tells us that God created "me and all creatures," but it gets more specific, telling us that God creates everyone as a gift imbued with dignity and worth, entrusts everyone with important gifts, calls everyone to use their gifts with purpose, expects everyone to grow and develop their gifts, and calls every church to equip people to use their gifts.

This good news about God the Father is so important for us to get right. When we neglect our biblical anthropology, we can treat ourselves and others without the dignity and respect we deserve as children of God.

But when we spend time hearing this good news, the implications are beautiful and several. As we've seen, understanding what the Bible says about how God created us has a natural way of

- confronting our low self-esteem,
- undercutting our habit of showing partiality,
- widening our too-narrow focus on spiritual gifts,
- helping people discover previously unnoticed gifts,
- broadening our celebration of calling,
- infusing everyday life with a sense of purpose,
- celebrating a developmental posture,
- reigniting gift development within the church,
- energizing local churches to unleash the gifts of the congregation, and
- reengaging local churches with their surrounding communities.

Perhaps that's not enough to do away with all division, distrust, and anxiety in our lives and churches, but it's an important start. And it's a step toward discovering, growing, and sharing every gift. Paul put it pretty simply:

> Having gifts that differ according to the grace given to us, let us use them. (Romans 12:6)

May it be so. May we see the gifts God has given each of us and rightly celebrate them. May we treat each other as the fearfully and wonderfully made gifts that we are.

And as we celebrate how God made us and everyone we know, may all kinds of hopeful paths open up before us.

Acknowledgments

While David's soul may have known very well how wonderful all of God's works are, my own soul knows very well how incomplete and naive and hackneyed my own works would be were it not for the generous help of a few groups of people.

And so, it is right to celebrate the many gifts generously shared with me by those who have shared their stories (especially Mark, Matthew, Gene, John, Dan, and Chris), those who've been a part of my own story (especially Buzz, Mom, Edilberto, Kevin, Rocky, Simon, Teya, Victor, Andy, Mary, AmyRuth, the purveyors of the Rabbit Room, and, of course, Wendy), the gifted crew at the Barna Group (especially David, Savannah, and Alyce), all of my partners at InterVarsity Press (especially Al), the amazing scholars and practitioners whose work I have built upon (Go read the endnotes, everyone!), and all of my friends and colleagues at Lutheran Hour Ministries.

You are, every last one of you, fearfully and wonderfully made. Your generosity has made this book what it is. Thank you.

Research Partners

Barna Group (barna.com) is a research firm dedicated to providing actionable insights on faith and culture, with a particular focus on the Christian church. Since 1984, Barna has conducted more than one million interviews in the course of hundreds of studies and has become a go-to source for organizations that want to better understand a complex and changing world from a faith perspective.

Lutheran Hour Ministries (lhm.org) is a trusted resource in global media that equips and engages a vibrant volunteer base to passionately proclaim the gospel to more than 150 million people worldwide each week. Through its North American headquarters and ministry centers on six continents, LHM reaches into more than fifty countries, often bringing Christ to places where no other Christian evangelistic organizations are present.

LHM and Barna are partnering on a multiyear research endeavor to reveal how Americans are expressing their faith. The first year of research looked at how individuals engage in spiritual conversations—for more on these findings you can read *The Reluctant Witness: Discovering the Delight of Spiritual Conversations*. The second year of research looked at the influence of households on spiritual development—see *The Spiritually Vibrant Home: The Power of Messy Prayers, Loud Tables, and Open Doors* for more on this study. The third year explored how Christians can be a welcome influence in their neighborhoods—read *The Hopeful Neighborhood: What Happens When Christians Pursue the Common Good* or *The Hopeful Neighborhood Field Guide* to learn more about our neighborhood research. Our fourth year of research, on which *Discover Your Gifts* is based, focuses on gifts.

Research Methodology

This quantitative study consisted of three online surveys. The first was a survey of 1,504 US adults with an oversample of 1,000 additional practicing Christians (meaning they self-identify as Christian, say their faith is very important in their life, and over the past year, on average, attended church at least one time per month). In total, responses from 1,374 practicing Christians were analyzed in this report. This survey was conducted from June 16 to July 6, 2020. The margin of error for the sample is +/- 2.3 percent for all US adults and +/- 2.5 percent for practicing Christians at the 95 percent confidence level.

The second quantitative survey focused on the twelve giftings explored within this publication and mastery measurements within giftings. This online survey was conducted among 1,019 US adults from September 3 through September 12, 2020. The margin of error for this sample is +/- 2.9 percent at the 95 percent confidence level.

For these two general population survey efforts, researchers set quotas to obtain a minimum readable sample by a variety of demographic factors and weighted the samples by region, ethnicity, education, age, and gender to reflect their natural presence in the American population (using US Census Bureau data and historical Barna data for comparison). Partly by nature of using an online panel, these respondents are slightly more educated than the average American, but Barna researchers adjusted the representation of college-educated individuals in the weighting scheme accordingly.

The third quantitative online survey was conducted among 491 US Protestant senior pastors from June 23 through July 28, 2020. These pastors were recruited from Barna's pastor panel (a database of pastors recruited via probability sampling on annual phone and email surveys) and are representative of US Protestant churches by region, denomination, and church size. The margin of error for this sample is +/- 4.4 percent at the 95 percent confidence level.[1]

Definitions

aware: Say they know or understand their own giftings, abilities, or skills "extremely" or "very" well (consists of 54% of practicing Christians, 46% of the general population)[1]

boomers: Born between 1946 and 1964

college degree: Earned a bachelor's degree, a graduate degree, or higher

custom segmentation: Growing in gifts: *Base: practicing Christian adults*

Gen X: Born between 1965 and 1983

Gen Z: Born between 1999 and 2015

high school or less: Attended grade school or high school or earned a high school diploma

high socioeconomic status: Adults with an annual household income of $75,000 or more and who do hold a college degree

low socioeconomic status: Adults with an annual household income of $20,000 or less and who do not hold a college degree

millennials: Born between 1984 and 1998

practicing Christians: Self-identified Christians who say their faith is very important in their lives and have attended a worship service within the past month

some college / trade school: Earned an associate degree, attended or graduated technical or vocational training, or attended college but did not graduate

The EveryGift Inventory

The **EveryGift Inventory** will help you discover the aptitudes, innate abilities, and acquired skills that make up your unique gifts in twelve distinct areas.

The inventory will take less than twenty minutes to complete and will provide you a personalized (absolutely free) overview of your gifts. To get started go to www.everygift.org.

Notes

INTRODUCTION

[1] Don Everts, *The Spiritually Vibrant Home: The Power of Messy Prayers, Loud Tables, and Open Doors* (Downers Grove, IL: InterVarsity Press, 2020).

[2] *Merriam-Webster,* s.v. "anthropology (*n.*)," accessed March 17, 2021, www.merriam-webster.com/dictionary/anthropology.

[3] Martin Luther, *Small Catechism*, First Article: Creation, accessed on August 26, 2021, https://catechism.cph.org/en/creed.html.

[4] Michael Downey, *A Blessed Weakness: The Spirit of Jean Vanier and l'Arche* (San Francisco: Harper & Row, 1986), 29.

[5] Gene Edward Veith Jr., *God at Work: Your Christian Vocation in All of Life* (Wheaton, IL: Crossway, 2002).

1 EVERYONE IS A GIFT

[1] Michael Downey, *A Blessed Weakness: The Spirit of Jean Vanier and l'Arche* (San Francisco: Harper & Row, 1986), 108.

[2] Downey, *A Blessed Weakness*, 110.

[3] C. S. Lewis, *The Weight of Glory and Other Addresses* (San Francisco: HarperOne, 2001), 47.

[4] Downey, *A Blessed Weakness*, 19. "Sacredness" here refers to the worth and value that people have as those created by God.

[5] When I refer to struggles with self-esteem, I am referring to how we understand ourselves as God's wonderfully created wonders. This psychological estimation of our created status is very different from our spiritual estimation of our legal status before God as fallen, sinful creatures. It is possible to proclaim with Psalm 139 that we are fearfully

and wonderfully made and simultaneously proclaim with Matthew 5:3 that we truly are poor in spirit.

[6]Barna Group, *Gifted for More: A Framework for Equipping Christians to Share Their Abilities and Skills in Everyday Life* (Ventura, CA: Barna, 2021), 24.

[7]Barna, *Gifted for More*, 22.

[8]Barna, *Gifted for More*, 24.

[9]Barna, *Gifted for More*, 24.

[10]Don Everts, *The Hopeful Neighborhood: What Happens When Christians Pursue the Common Good* (Downers Grove, IL: InterVarsity Press, 2020), 30.

[11]Don Everts, *The Reluctant Witness: Discovering the Delight of Spiritual Conversations* (Downers Grove, IL: InterVarsity Press, 2019), 36.

[12]Barna Group, *Spiritual Conversations in the Digital Age: How Christians' Approach to Sharing Their Faith Has Changed in 25 Years* (Ventura, CA: Barna, 2018), 63.

[13]"What Millennials Want When They Visit Church," Barna Research, March 4, 2015, www.barna.com/research/what-millennials-want-when -they-visit-church.

2 EVERYONE HAS GIFTS

[1]John Calvin, *Calvin: The Institutes of the Christian Religion*, ed. John T. McNeill (Philadelphia: Westminster, 1960), 2.2.14.

[2]Victor P. Hamilton, *The New International Commentary on the Old Testament: The Book of Genesis: Chapters 1-17* (Grand Rapids, MI: Eerdmans, 1990), 171.

[3]Amy L. Sherman, *Kingdom Calling: Vocational Stewardship for the Common Good* (Downers Grove, IL: InterVarsity Press, 2011), 20.

[4]Timothy Keller and Katherine Leary Alsdorf, *Every Good Endeavor: Connecting Your Work to God's Work* (New York: Penguin, 2012), 190.

[5]Barna Group, *Gifted for More: A Framework for Equipping Christians to Share Their Abilities and Skills in Everyday Life* (Ventura, CA: Barna, 2021), 109.

[6]Barna, *Gifted for More*, 109.

[7]Barna, *Gifted for More*, 113.

[8]Barna, *Gifted for More*, 111.

[9]Gene Edward Veith Jr, *God at Work: Your Christian Vocation in All of Life* (Wheaton, IL: Crossway, 2002), 52.

[10]Barna, *Gifted for More*, 22.

[11]Barna, *Gifted for More*, 21.

[12]Barna, *Gifted for More*, June 13–July 6, 2020 quantitative survey. See appendix two.

[13]Katelyn Beaty, *A Woman's Place: A Christian Vision for Your Calling in the Office, the Home, and the World* (New York: Howard Books, 2016); and Margot Starbuck, *Unsqueezed: Springing Free from Skinny Jeans, Nose Jobs, Highlights, and Stilettos* (Downers Grove, IL: InterVarsity Press, 2010).

[1e]Barna, *Gifted for More*, 20.

[1r]Barna, *Gifted for More*, 20.

[15]Barna, *Gifted for More*, 109.

[16]Barna, *Gifted for More*, 110.

3 EVERYONE IS CALLED

[1]Gene Edward Veith Jr., *God at Work: Your Christian Vocation in All of Life* (Wheaton, IL: Crossway, 2002), 19.

[2]Martin Luther, "The Gospel for the Early Christmas Service," trans. John G. Kunstmann, *Luther's Works*, vol. 52 (Philadelphia: Fortress, 1974), 36-38.

[3]Timothy Keller and Katherine Leary Alsdorf, *Every Good Endeavor: Connecting Your Work to God's Work* (New York: Penguin, 2012), 54-55.

[4]Keller and Alsdorf, *Every Good Endeavor*, 55.

[5]Gene Edward Veith Jr., *Working for Our Neighbor: A Lutheran Primer on Vocation, Economics, and Ordinary Life* (Grand Rapids, MI: Christian's Library Press, 2016), xv.

[6]Keller and Alsdorf, *Every Good Endeavor*, 22.

[7]Keller and Alsdorf, *Every Good Endeavor*, 23.

[8]Ben Witherington III, *Work: A Kingdom Perspective on Labor* (Grand Rapids, MI: Eerdmans, 2011), 2.

[9]Keller and Alsdorf, *Every Good Endeavor*, 43.

[10]Walter Brueggemann, "Mentoring in the Old Testament," in *Biblical, Theological, and Practical Perspectives*, ed. Dean K. Thompson and D. Cameron Murchison (Grand Rapids, MI: Eerdmans, 2018), 8.

[11]Veith, *Working for Our Neighbor*, xii.

[12]William C. Placher, *Callings: Twenty Centuries of Christian Wisdom on Vocation* (Grand Rapids, MI: Eerdmans, 2005), 206.

[13]Al Hsu, "Is All Work a High Calling?", *The High Calling* (blog), December 19, 2013, www.patheos.com/blogs/thehighcalling/2013/12/is-all-work-a-high-calling.

[14]Martin Luther, "The Estate of Marriage," trans. Walther I. Brandt, *Luther's Works*, vol. 45 (Philadelphia: Muhlenberg, 1962), 40.

[15]Keller and Alsdorf, *Every Good Endeavor*, 35.

[16]Keller and Alsdorf, *Every Good Endeavor*, 37.

[17]Keller and Alsdorf, *Every Good Endeavor*, 64.

[18]Barna Group, *Gifted for More: A Framework for Equipping Christians to Share Their Abilities and Skills in Everyday Life* (Ventura, CA: Barna, 2021), 82.

[19]Barna, *Gifted for More*, 85.

[20]Barna, *Gifted for More*, 63.

[21]Gene Edward Veith Jr., *God at Work: Your Christian Vocation in All of Life* (Wheaton, IL: Crossway, 2002), 16.

[22]Placher, *Callings*, 1.

[23]Placher, *Callings*, 3.

[24]Hugh Whelchel, *How Then Should We Work?: Rediscovering the Biblical Doctrine of Work* (McLean, VA: Institute for Faith, Work & Economics), xxiii.

[25]Barna, *Gifted for More*, 87.

[26]One notable demographic standout was among Black Americans; they are significantly more likely to "agree strongly" that they feel able to make good use of—or apply—their giftings (38% vs. 22% White, 26% Hispanic, 13% Asian).

[27]Barna, *Gifted for More*, 43.

4 EVERYONE CAN GROW

[1]You can find out more about their small company, the Adriel Collective, by going to www.adrielcollective.com.

[2]Walter Brueggemann, "Mentoring in the Old Testament," in *Biblical, Theological, and Practical Perspectives*, ed. Dean K. Thompson and D. Cameron Murchison (Grand Rapids, MI: Eerdmans, 2018), 21.

[3]Paul Stanley and Robert Clinton, *Connecting: The Mentoring Relationships You Need to Succeed in Life* (Colorado Springs, CO: NavPress, 2014), 17.

[4]Brueggemann, "Mentoring," 2.

[5]François Fénelon, *The Adventures of Telemachus, the Son of Ulysses*, trans. Tobias Smollett (Athens: University of Georgia Press, 2014), 17.

[6]Stanley and Clinton, *Connecting*, 222.

[7]Stanley and Clinton, *Connecting*, 215.

[8]Stanley and Clinton, *Connecting*, 222.

[9]Barna Group, *Gifted for More: A Framework for Equipping Christians to Share Their Abilities and Skills in Everyday Life* (Ventura, CA: Barna, 2021), 65.

[10]Barna, *Gifted for More*, 38.

[11]Barna, *Gifted for More*, June 16–July 6, 2020 quantitative survey, see appendix two.

[12]Barna, *Gifted for More*, 48.

[13]Barna, *Gifted for More*, 68.

[14]Stanley and Clinton, *Connecting*, 17.

[15]Stanley and Clinton, *Connecting*, 18.

[16]Barna, *Gifted for More*, 58.

[17]Barna, *Gifted for More*, 88.

[18]Barna, *Gifted for More*, 42.

[19]Barna, *Gifted for More*, 49, 52.

[20]Barna, *Gifted for More*, 39.

[21]Barna, *Gifted for More*, 46.

[22]Barna, *Gifted for More*, 63.

5 EVERY CHURCH CAN EQUIP

[1]Second Epistle of Barnabas 4.10, as cited in Michael Lamb and Brian A. Williams, eds., *Everyday Ethics: Moral Theology and the Practices of Ordinary Life* (Washington, DC: Georgetown University Press, 2019), 145.

[2]Christopher Wright, *The Mission of God: Unlocking the Bible's Grand Narrative* (Downers Grove, IL: IVP Academic, 2006), 63.

[3]Lesslie Newbigin as quoted in Michael Frost, *The Road to Missional: Journey to the Center of the Church* (Grand Rapids, MI: Baker, 2011), 104.

[4]David Bosch as quoted in Michael Frost, *The Road to Missional: Journey to the Center of the Church* (Grand Rapids, MI: Baker, 2011), 24.

[5]J. D. Hunter, *To Change the World* (New York: Oxford University Press, 2010), 277.

[6]Don Everts, *Go and Do: Becoming a Missional Christian* (Downers Grove, IL: InterVarsity Press, 2012), 128.

[7]Gene Edward Veith Jr., *Working for Our Neighbor: A Lutheran Primer on Vocation, Economics, and Ordinary Life* (Grand Rapids, MI: Christian's Library Press, 2016), 104.

[8]Everts, *Go and Do*, 128.

[9]Everts, *Go and Do*, 128.

[10]Amy Sherman, *Kingdom Calling: Vocational Stewardship for the Common Good* (Downers Grove, IL: InterVarsity Press, 2011), 21.

[11]Barna Group, *Gifted for More: A Framework for Equipping Christians to Share Their Abilities and Skills in Everyday Life* (Ventura, CA: Barna, 2021), 47.

[12]Barna, *Gifted for More*, 111.

[13]Barna, *Gifted for More*, 110.

[14]Barna, *Gifted for More*, 25, 61, 84.

[15]Barna, *Gifted for More*, 112.

[16]Barna, *Gifted for More*, 112.

[17]Barna, *Gifted for More*, 60.

[18]Barna, *Gifted for More*, 25.

[19]Barna, *Gifted for More*, 60.

[20]Sherman, *Kingdom Calling*, 21.

[21]Don Everts, *The Hopeful Neighborhood: What Happens When Christians Pursue the Common Good* (Downers Grove, IL: InterVarsity Press, 2020).

[22]Hunter, *To Change the World*, 276.

[23]Sherman, *Kingdom Calling*, 151.

[24]Barna, *Gifted for More*, 84.

[25]Barna, *Gifted for More*, 112.

[26]Barna, *Gifted for More*, 63.

[27]Barna, *Gifted for More*, 98.

[28]Barna, *Gifted for More*, 100.

[29]Barna, *Gifted for More*, 99.

APPENDIX 2: RESEARCH METHODOLOGY

[1]Barna Group, *Gifted for More: A New Framework for Equipping Christians to Share Their Abilities and Skills in Everyday Life* (Ventura, CA: Barna, 2021), 140.

APPENDIX 3: DEFINITIONS

[1]These definitions are from Barna Group, *Gifted for More: A New Framework for Equipping Christians to Share Their Abilities and Skills in Everyday Life* (Ventura, CA: Barna, 2021), 143.

THE **HOPEFUL NEIGHBORHOOD PROJECT** ®

The Hopeful Neighborhood Project is a collaborative network committed to improving neighborhood well-being around the world. Our resources and online network equip and encourage neighbors to work together, using their gifts and the gifts of their community, to pursue the common good of their neighborhood.

To find out more about our
active network and many resources visit us at
hopefulneighborhood.org.

Also Available

Discover Your Gifts Workbook
978-1-5140-0449-4

Other Titles by Don Everts

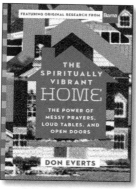

The Spiritually Vibrant Home
978-0-8308-4590-3

The Reluctant Witness
978-0-8308-4567-5

The Hopeful Neighborhood
978-0-8308-4803-4

**The Hopeful Neighborhood
Field Guide**
978-0-8308-4732-7